LIFE LINES
Verses for Reflection and Recovery

written and illustrated by

JAN SHAW KING

Collection of Inspirational Verses

with Original Watercolor Illustrations

imprint of WBE Global LLC

LIFE LINES
Verses for Reflection and Recovery

WHAT PEOPLE ARE SAYING ABOUT THIS BOOK...

TESTIMONIALS

"I am so moved by your verses in <u>LIFE LINES</u>. As a now 3-year Breast Cancer survivor, the fog is clearing, and psychological healing is taking place. Your words speak to me and to so many of us moving through this healing process. Thank you so much for sharing your journey with the world. Your words reach out with validation, care and comfort to move us through this journey.
~ Kathy Radocaj, R.N. (ret.) Pediatric Oncology, Cancer Survivor

"<u>LIFE LINES: Verses for Reflection and Recovery</u> is very inspirational and moving. I know it will uplift others who are struggling, especially women. Great job!"
~ Barb T., R.N.

"I read your prolific poetry and enjoyed it all. It is strong and supportive content for many to use for their own journeys to help weather their storms and overcome the obstacles and challenges that life puts in front of them. They are so well done, deeply descriptive and capture your every emotion. This book will help many people, as you have overcome your trials and tribulations. Of course, I am a big fan of your art. It is lovely".
~ F. Scott Moyer, Music Educator, Composer, Accident Victim

"The powerful beauty of <u>LIFE LINES: Verses for Reflection and Recovery</u> transported me emotionally in a healing zone. I saw each treatment as a steppingstone to the top of the mountain when I was combating enemy cells. And now, I will share with others who will benefit from its essence. Wonderful!"
~ Bonnye R., Cancer Conqueror; One-year clear Survivor!

"You are an answer to my prayers! Thank you so much for sharing your book with me. After reading the first few pages, I am already blessed. God is good and faithful, and I am trying to keep my focus on Him and my many blessings. Thank you for walking with me in this season.
~ Archdeacon, Julia R. Recovering from Surgery

"Your most heartfelt and heartwarming book, <u>LIFE LINES: Verses for Reflection and Recovery</u>, is magnificent! Every word touched my heart. Thank you.
God is wonderful! **~ Marcia Allers, Medical Assistant, Caregiver**

DEDICATION

SPECIAL THANKS

A special thanks to my wonderful husband

for his love, guidance, support and comfort,

to my children, family, friends, and my doctors.

To everyone who will travel with me on this journey,

go with love and peace, with a grand sense of

adventure, humor, and a forgiving and tender heart.

Be happy - Be well - Be blessed.

For you are a beacon of Hope!

Go forth – Live your Life!

Namaste

~ Jan Shaw King

FORWARD

It has been my honor to read this book and enjoy both the creative art and the beautifully written verses that accompany the paintings.

As the co-creator of the Healing Odyssey Retreat experience, I am so pleased that many years later, Jan can recall and credit her retreat experience with gaining strength for her personal cancer journey.

This book is filled with wonderful original art, personal reflections in deeply personal verses, and the open space to allow for survivors to express their own thoughts and feelings. This book can help anyone by giving hope to those facing losses in personal life and in their health challenges.

I plan to provide copies of this book to other cancer survivors as it can be an important tool in their cancer journey. I especially appreciate the personal expressions of gratitude and spirituality, which are so important as we grow through life's challenging moments.

~ Donna Farris, LCSWP

CONTENTS

ABOUT HEALING ODYSSEY

"Healing Odyssey is about empowering women cancer survivors to be strong, hopeful and courageous."* The program offers a weekend of extraordinary opportunities in a mountain retreat setting to learn self-healing tools and new coping skills to empower women to meet the challenges of a cancer diagnosis, treatment and recovery toward health. Through experiential learning, trust building, teamwork and self-exploration activities, women learn new life coping tools and regain a sense of personal power. Healing Odyssey is a place where women can begin to acknowledge their feelings and discover untapped abilities. In a setting of breathtaking beauty and serenity, away from the pressures of daily life, participants begin to more effectively face some of life's most demanding challenges. The intensive nature of this weekend experience encourages the formation of deep friendships, which may continue after they've returned home.

The Healing Odyssey retreats began in May 1994 and have been held semi-annually in the Spring and Fall at Rancho La Sherpa, north of Santa Barbara, California. The retreat was created to go beyond the typical support group experience offering life changing learning opportunities to help women deal with the challenges of illness and their recovery to health. Designed to complement traditional medical treatment, the Healing Odyssey retreat utilizes dynamic teaching techniques of experiential learning.

*A quote from Healing Odyssey, A Weekend Retreat for Women Cancer Survivors

Healing Odyssey's Leaders, include:

Healing Odyssey Co-Founder, President
Donna Farris, M.S.W., L.C.S.W., Clinical Social Worker

Healing Odyssey Co-Founder:
Nancy Raymon, R.N, M.N, A.O.C.N, Oncology Nurse Specialist

Bill John, President/Co-Founder
Ropes Course Specialist, personal and team development.
Odyssey Performance Enhancement Network, Inc.

Jan Shaw (Szymanski) King is a graduate of HO9, Healing Odyssey 1998.
As Survivor, Jan walked the Relay for Life by the American Cancer Society in Los Angeles, CA, and earned a gold medal for completing the course.

www.healingodyssey.net

ABOUT THE AUTHOR-ILLUSTRATOR

JAN SHAW KING

Jan Shaw King is a cancer survivor and loves life! She is an Artist, Illustrator, successful Producer, Writer, Director of film and television, an accomplished project Design Developer, Creative Executive for Themed Entertainment, a professional Acrylic, Watercolorist and Children's Author-Illustrator. She holds Painting Workshops on location and online.

After raising three children in Upstate New York, Jan relocated to Orlando, Florida where she was producing and directing TV series. Upon being offered a production position for a motion picture, Jan moved to Los Angeles, California in 1997. Prior to moving, Jan was in extreme pain, and was misdiagnosed.

Almost immediately upon arrival in LA, Jan was diagnosed with Sarcoma, an aggressive form of uterine and ovarian cancer that was life threatening with approximately one month to live if the cancer was not removed immediately. After two back-to-back surgeries and painful, aggressive radiation treatments at Cedar Sinai Hospital, Jan fully recovered due to her doctors giving her faith. She was told she would be 100% cured within two years. After her five-year checkup, her doctor told her she was a miracle in that her form of cancer was so rare and aggressive that her doctors thought she had one month to live, and if she lived more than six months, or one year, it would be a miracle. By her doctors telling her she would be 100% cured, it gave her hope to reach toward living a long, happy life for her children and future grandchildren, and a future love who would share the rest of her life.

Six months prior to her cancer diagnosis, Jan's adventurous spirit faced challenges head-on, by successfully navigating 75-miles down the Chatanika River, by canoe, in the Alaskan wilderness. While riding horseback up a 10,000-foot mountain in Colorado with one of her sons, they came across a giant herd of over 100-Elk at the summit.

Those arduous experiences built her confidence to believe that she could do anything. They prepared her to courageously face cancer after she was diagnosed, by envisioning being in the mountains, well and fit again, and through tough times while she was completely on her own.

After her long and difficult recovery process, Jan attended the Healing Odyssey weekend, a retreat for women cancer survivors at Rancho La Sherpa, north of Santa Barbara, California. It was during the retreat that Jan learned new ways to face her fears and regain her confidence. The support from other women cancer survivors was a powerful experience by sharing fellowship and new life skills. The experiences Jan had, the friendships she made with other remarkably strong, powerful women cancer survivors, and family and friends who supported her, truly became her "Life Lines". Jan found solace in writing inspirational verses, and painting watercolors and acrylics. Twenty-seven years later, she published her inspirational verses for others to benefit from her experiences.

As a professional Acrylic Artist and Watercolorist, Jan exhibited her work in several galleries, art shows and national competitions. She won many awards and ribbons for her work. In *LIFE LINES: Verses for Reflection and Recovery,* Jan's original impressionistic watercolor paintings embrace the beauty of life. They complement Jan's collection of verses, a body of work that celebrates the joy of life, and inspires people to face their own life challenges with courage. Her verses extend a message of hope and encouragement to celebrate their uniqueness, connectedness, the human spirit, and faith in God's purpose for each of us on our journey.

Jan found her calling as an Artist. As an Environmental Naturalist, to promote awareness, Jan is painting a series of Endangered Species, including, Sea Turtles, marine life and wildlife who have been affected by climate change, and the real dangers of becoming extinct. By painting these magnificent animals, Jan's mission is to support rescue and rehabilitation of endangered and critically endangered species for them to survive long into the future, free from extinction. Jan resides in Orlando, Florida working with her Author-Illustrator husband on publishing a variety of book titles.

Expression Page

To encourage and inspire you to express your own thoughts, feelings, and what a verse means to you on your own road to recovery, an Expression page is positioned opposite each verse, reserved for you to write your comments, thoughts, notes, journal, or your own verses.

"Dunes with Snow Fence, Harwich Beach", Cape Cod, MA"
15" x 30" Watercolor, © 1996 Jan Shaw King

I love painting *en plein air*, especially on the beach, brushed by salty sea breezes and sounds of the ocean surrounding me, where I feel a sense of peace and serenity. I chose a section of one of my favorite series of Cape Cod Dunes watercolors for the background of the Expression page, to create a safe, serene space for your personal use.

WHY I CHOSE THIS PAINTING FOR THE COVER

"Meditation Mount Summit, Ojai, CA"
22" x 15" Watercolor, © Jan Shaw King 1998

Meditation Mount is a special, spiritual space, perched on top of a mountain overlooking Ojai, CA with awe-inspiring views of the Pacific Ocean. It is a serene, healing place where worship and ceremonial tributes take place. Millenniums ago, Native Americans viewed this summit as a holy place. Carved lines on the mountain opposite this site mark sunsets at various times of the year, serving as a seasonal calendar. After my surgeries, a good friend introduced me to this site to meditate. These chairs were positioned overlooking a small pond as if to beckon me to sit and meditate with God by my side. This was a special healing place where I had returned to many times.

PROLOGUE

Dramatic milestone events have tremendous impact on our lives. On the surface, those events appear to be circumstantial, that they just happen. The difficult challenges we face in times of adversity sometimes take all of our strength to endure. However, until we are faced with adversity, we will not realize our true potential, our spirit, courage, and inner strength that we possess, or appreciate how wonderful and beautiful life truly is. In hindsight, when we emerge from the fire, we realize that life's challenges and upheavals are about change and growth. Although unplanned and unexpected, challenges enlighten our lives with new beginnings and a new perspective. They alter our perception of life in more fulfilling ways. When we are open to learning from our experiences, we transition into grace by sharing our experiences with others, which enrich other people's lives and guide them along their paths. When my life was in upheaval, I began writing down my thoughts and feelings in order to cope. My life was filled with confusion, anguish, and anxiety. And yet, I clung to a bright light filled with a hopeful future. As I wrote down my thoughts, what transpired profoundly surprised me. I discovered a new creative side of myself that was lurking within as a Poet, exploding onto paper in the form of inspirational verses. As an Author-Illustrator, my writer friends encouraged me to continue to paint with words, if only for the exercise. As I transitioned from one life experience to another, my writings revealed my perception of life around me. I realized that my verses became a powerful source of personal healing energy and fulfillment, not only for myself, but for others, as well. Inspirational verses arose from my innermost thoughts and feelings of love, despair, hope, and courage into joyful, creative, and healing energy.

LIFE LINES: Verses for Reflection and Recovery is a body of work that originally represented my personal self-discovery and evolution. However, the next step of the connection process was the impact that these verses had for others. Many, who have read my verses, have encouraged me to continue to write and reach out to people for healing in one commonality. As an Artist, I embrace the creative process. The creation of a work of art comes from the infusion of heart, mind, and passionate soul that is embodied into an art form. In order to complete the process of artistic expression, a miracle must occur. The true essence of art is fully realized when it connects and inspires the reader, or viewer, and is received in a profound way.

After recovering from my cancer surgeries and radiation treatments, I attended Healing Odyssey Weekend Retreat for Women Cancer Survivors near Santa Barbara, California. It is a beautiful semi-annual event where women refuge in the mountains to meditate, support one another, face their fears, hug each other, hold each other's hand, heal and bond their souls and spirits together. During the retreat, I shared some of my verses to offer hope and inspiration. From their positive reaction, I soon discovered that my work had a profound purpose. What began as a healing process for me, became a collection of verses to be shared as a source of inspiration and healing for others. While I was going through tough times, I was unable to paint. After attending Healing Odyssey, I slowly began to heal, pick up a brush again and illustrate the paintings for LIFE LINES: Verses for Reflections and Recovery to share with other cancer survivors, people with illnesses, surgeries, accidents, or other life challenges. Like a butterfly, I emerged from my cocoon, unfolded my wings, and flew.

This body of work is a compilation of messages of love and hope. It is my ultimate wish that my writings will inspire people, to impact their lives during their own journeys, self-discovery, and healing process toward positive, happy, and spiritually fulfilling lives.

Let the journey begin. Namaste.

~ Jan Shaw King

"Castle Rock on Table Mountain, Golden, CO"
20" x 14" Watercolor, © 2016 Jan Shaw King

When I held one of my Watercolor Workshops in Golden, Colorado, I painted Castle Rock on Table Mountain, a prominent site overlooking the historic town of Golden, which I used on my Poster. To me, it represents the pinnacle of strength and perseverance to overcome life's challenges.

Expression Page

_____

I BELIEVE

I believe I can do anything.

I believe in my strength,

    ...my courage,

    ...my persistence,

    ...my will to endure,

    ...and my beauty as a human being.

I believe in myself.

    ...I am determined,

    ...I am focused,

    ...I will reach my goals,

    ...and I will overcome adversity.

Expression Page

_____
_____
_____
_____
_____
_____
_____
_____
_____
_____
_____
_____
_____
_____
_____
_____
_____
_____
_____
_____
_____
_____
_____
_____
_____

THE FOOTBRIDGE OF LIFE*

I face the unknown.

I stare bold-faced, stubbornly challenging the future.
A little voice inside me cries and mourns the losses.
It remembers all too well the past and its pain.
I panic with uncertainly as I step tentatively
Across the wavering footbridge.
I cling to the ropes, clutching my lifeline.

But I will be fine. I will survive.
I plan each step carefully along the way, plotting my course
Using maps of instinct and my compass
Of common sense to guide me.
I make sure the footbridge is strongly secured on the other side.
I will cross the caverns of life with dignity
And a sense of adventure.

And I will follow these guidelines:

Do not look down with dread,
But marvel instead at the massive streams
And waterfalls below me, brimming with life.

Do not look out to the vastness spread before me in fear
As I quake in my aloneness.
But know that I am one with God's Universe
That I share the wonder of Creation, of which I am one.

Do not freeze at the crossing of unsteady bridges
Insecure of the unknown that lies ahead
But anticipate the future before me as an Adventure
Packed with marvelous awakenings, fresh new beginnings
And an exciting exploration of Life.

© 1998 Jan Shaw King

* *I wrote this verse after walking across a log positioned 15 ft off the ground
 as part of an adventure challenge course. (and yes, I had a harness on!)*

Expression Page

_____
_____
_____
_____
_____
_____
_____
_____
_____
_____
_____
_____
_____
_____
_____
_____
_____
_____
_____
_____
_____
_____
_____
_____
_____
_____
_____
_____
_____

THE COMPASS

How do I manage this thing called Life?
How do I take on this Journey, this cold apparition
That haunts me at every turn
With promises of magic and illusion?

Where will this path lead me?
Every twist of fate, every destiny.
My choices wind through every turn.
What outcome will become me in the end?

I can only come to one conclusion.
After much soul searching
My life's compass rests on decisions
Manufactured from within.

The choice is mine alone.
I must listen to my heart
For there the truth remains in my center of existence
My internal map that leads me home.

© 1998 Jan Shaw King

Expression Page

_____
_____
_____
_____
_____
_____
_____
_____
_____
_____
_____
_____
_____
_____
_____
_____
_____
_____
_____
_____
_____
_____
_____
_____
_____
_____

MY GARDEN OF LIFE

My children and friends are my greatest asset.
They fill my treasure chest of life.
They are windows to my soul, mirrors reflecting
The best of my inner being, heart and soul.
They are my kindred spirits, unconditionally
Understanding and accepting of all that I am.
I am their rock in times of insecurity,
Their strength during earthquakes and mudslides,
And they are mine.

They are an eclectic mix of talents, temperaments,
Personalities, beauty, and wonder.
They represent all that I strive to be:

...Intelligent, worldly, energetic, humorous,
...Poetic, honest, sensitive, imaginative, assertive,
...Loyal and devoted, compassionate and giving.

Although they have been loaned to me for a moment,
They are like flowers in a garden that I will
Cherish, nurture, care for, guide, protect, defend,
Warm with radiant sunshine,
And shower with all my love and friendship,
Unconditionally...

...Forever.

© 1997 Jan Shaw King

Expression Page

_____
_____
_____
_____
_____
_____
_____
_____
_____
_____
_____
_____
_____
_____
_____
_____
_____
_____
_____
_____
_____
_____
_____
_____
_____
_____

CHAINS

My shackles and chains cut deep
Wrapped tightly around my ankles so I can't run
Around my wrists so I can't reach out
Squeezed around my neck,
Choking me so I can't breathe.

Beaten and bludgeoned by words
That sear through my being,
I am bound and harnessed by paper.

But my mind and soul are free.
My spirit soars.

Each link on the chain becomes the joy of life:
A beautiful flower, the innocence of a baby bird
My wondrous child, a tender touch of a loving friend.

The chains on my wrists crumble as I reach out.
Helping others in their crisis heals my wounds.
My friends cradle me in their arms.

Forgiveness comes hard.
The links on my neck chain are rusted with time.
Some scars may never heal.
The brittle links break away.

Ankle chains don't come cheap.
Made of paper and coin, each chain weighs a ton.
The lock is secure.

Time, faith, courage, hope and trust
Are my friends who will heal the scars.

Fire of determination crackle at my feet.
Someday my ankle chains will burn and set me free.

I long for that day.

Expression Page

_____
_____
_____
_____
_____
_____
_____
_____
_____
_____
_____
_____
_____
_____
_____
_____
_____
_____
_____
_____
_____
_____
_____
_____
_____
_____

MY "SELF"

I reach out ~
But I can't touch you.

I speak ~
But you don't hear me.

I cry out your name ~
But you don't know me.

I long to hold you ~
But you've vanished from my arms.

How can I reach you
When you're no longer here?

Like a phantom, you've disappeared.

My heart aches
And my soul cries sorrowful tears.
My lover is lost.

Only Faith keeps this love alive.

When my phantom returns
To be reborn,
Loving and living Life.

© 1997 Jan Shaw King

Expression Page

_____
_____
_____
_____
_____
_____
_____
_____
_____
_____
_____
_____
_____
_____
_____
_____
_____
_____
_____
_____
_____
_____
_____
_____
_____
_____
_____
_____

TALENTS

Talents are precious gifts
Tenderly tucked within
By our loving Father,
Magnificent gifts,
Wrapped and packaged with care.

Respect the Gift-giver.
Be grateful for His generosity and vision.
We are His messengers that complete His work.

His gift comes with only one set of instructions:
Nurture your talents and guard them like jewels.
Then share them generously with others.

For Talents are precious gifts
Gently loaned to us
By our loving Father
For us to give to others in return.

© 1998 Jan Shaw King

Expression Page

_____
_____
_____
_____
_____
_____
_____
_____
_____
_____
_____
_____
_____
_____
_____
_____
_____
_____
_____
_____
_____
_____
_____
_____
_____
_____
_____

THE THIEF

Death comes quickly to some
And slowly for others,
While some of the living
Die a slow death
When they don't live life to the fullest.

The joy of living comes from the heart
Savoring each day, daring to take risks,
Sharing God-given talents,
Touching the hearts and souls
Of others along the way.

When we give much of ourselves
We remain alive in so many memories.

Celebrate the joy of living.
Become fulfilled and radiate to others
Culminating through the passage
Of an eternal Grace.

© 1997 Jan Shaw King

Expression Page

_____
_____
_____
_____
_____
_____
_____
_____
_____
_____
_____
_____
_____
_____
_____
_____
_____
_____
_____
_____
_____
_____
_____
_____
_____
_____

MY CHILD

I was blessed
When the Lord's hand touched my womb
And filled me with supreme happiness
At great anticipation of your birth.

When you were born
The wonder and miracle of you
Filled my heart
With a love I had never known.

I thanked the Lord
And promised to cherish you
And always take care of you
Raise you into a strong, fine person.

I would love you
And teach you to love others.
I would fight for you
But not fight your battles.
I would hold you
But slowly let you go.
I would care for you
But show you how to care for yourself.
I would teach you
But not stifle your curiosity.
I would encourage you
To reach out and grab the world for your own.

Fortunately, I did not know what a challenge
The Lord placed into my hands.
What a difficult task lay ahead.
But my love for you was strong,
And I knew I would overcome any obstacle.
I was put to the ultimate test
A countless number of times,
But I held on.

~ continued

Expression Page

_____
_____
_____
_____
_____
_____
_____
_____
_____
_____
_____
_____
_____
_____
_____
_____
_____
_____
_____
_____
_____
_____
_____
_____
_____

MY CHILD (continued)

I was there for you
When you could not be there for yourself.
And I believed in you
When you struggled to believe in yourself.
One day, you would come through your internal turmoil
And be whole.

I blinked
And those years have vanished
Locked in my memory for all time.

The Lord gave me a miracle
To nurture and borrow for awhile.
Now it is time to let go
To watch you stand on your own
Proud, strong, and independent
To rediscover the world,
To challenge the universe
And make it your own.

Part of me grieves for the loss of my child
The fun we used to share together
Your curiosity,
The wonder of the world when you were small,
And your all-knowing when you were growing up.

But I am most proud and extremely happy
As I see you standing before me as a young adult,
A good, honest, kind, considerate, generous person
One who I would be proud to call my friend.

You will always be part of me
As I am part of you
Forever.

You are truly wonderful.
I am filled with supreme happiness,
Great joy and anticipation
As I watch you take charge of your life!

© 1997 Jan Shaw King

Expression Page

_____
_____
_____
_____
_____
_____
_____
_____
_____
_____
_____
_____
_____
_____
_____
_____
_____
_____
_____
_____
_____
_____
_____
_____
_____

THE CHALLENGE

The selfish thief tiptoes through the night
And casts aside my dignity
Robbing me of personal fulfillment
As though it means nothing,
Tossing aside my heart and soul.

What madness is this, this stark apparition?
How dare he claim my internal desires?
Parchment does not give him the right to own me
Nor the right to extinguish my fires.

Leaving behind the grand dream of illusions
Of family, happy hearth and home,
A woman's core essence is to love and to nurture.
It is hard to strike out alone.

Without true love, intimacy, connection and a purpose to share,
Then where lies a future if there is nothing left
But a chewed up, leathery heart
That if left unattended, will dry up and die?

I must preserve what is left, live life to its fullest
If it means loving completely in spite of it all.
Am I a fool who will stand cold in the future
Looking back on this tragedy?

Or do I contain the romance that is within,
The fantasy, my essence, the beauty of life,
The magic that drives me, my sense of well-being
My beauty mark that keeps me whole?

This capsule, this vessel, this body and soul
Must hold onto what is beautiful and true
For my dignity, my self-worth, to make my mark
And contribute all that I am.

The map has been drawn; the chart has been cast.
My life's purpose must strike out anew
With God's grace and blessing to fulfill my destiny,
With heavy heart, mixed with anticipation.

I meet Life's challenge. © 1997 Jan Shaw King

Expression Page

_____

_____

_____

_____

_____

_____

_____

_____

_____

_____

_____

_____

_____

_____

_____

_____

_____

_____

_____

_____

_____

_____

_____

_____

"Dunes with Sea Oats, Anna Maria Island, Florida"
Watercolor 21" X 28", © 2016 Jan Shaw King

BEACH DREAMS

Waves crashing 'round me,
Scattered in seafoam
Washing away my fears
Erasing my scars so no one will notice
The battered and lonely years.

Digging my toes in wet sand eternal
Making my mark set in time.
Restless within this scene of tranquility
Nothing can shatter my mind.

Clutching forever, my heart and my soul
The essence of all that I am,
Gliding through this new rite of passage
As the sea carves paths through the sand.

Freedom cries skyward on seagull's wing
Calling and beckoning me
Soon I will wade out past the tide
To take on the wide, open sea.

Sharks all around me with wide, gaping jaws
Vermin in the darkness unseen.
Eels and claws slashing my ankles
Hungry and tenaciously mean.

Gentle hands lift me to new horizons.
Your strength brings me safely to shore.
Hold me close, my friend for a lifetime
To cherish forevermore.

Running and laughing, kicking up sand
Sharing and bonding our souls.
Sweet salty breezes brush past our lips
Broken hearts now become whole.

Grasp my coral, pearly-white conch shell
Hold tightly against your ear
Hear waves of abandon,
Carving through time
And know that I am always near.

© 1998 Jan Shaw King

Expression Page

_____
_____
_____
_____
_____
_____
_____
_____
_____
_____
_____
_____
_____
_____
_____
_____
_____
_____
_____
_____
_____
_____
_____
_____
_____
_____

TAKE A CHANCE ON LIFE

Nothing becomes nothing
Empty and gray, void of feeling, free of pain
Fearful of ridicule and despair
Afraid to take a chance.

Embrace Life.
Stare it down when it takes its toll.
Grab onto its tenuous tendrils.
Do not let it slip from your grasp.

Dare to love and live Life.
Shine in the light of each moment.
Hold onto each fleeting second.
Make the most of your journey.

Travel through Life carefully.
Do not waste each precious life force.
Safely step through the door of chance
With a deep awareness of truth.

Open your senses
Follow your heart light.
Welcome the newness of the unfamiliar
That will shape your existence.

Smile and breathe through your soul.
This is why you came to be.

Live Life!

Love Life!

© 1998 Jan Shaw King

Expression Page

_____
_____
_____
_____
_____
_____
_____
_____
_____
_____
_____
_____
_____
_____
_____
_____
_____
_____
_____
_____
_____
_____
_____
_____
_____

CREATIVITY

When in the course of our human existence
Comes a moment of recognition
An awakening of our consciousness
That breathes life into our soul.

Our creative instincts manifest into wondrous miracles.
Every thought pattern, every wave of emotion
Join forces with our cosmic experience
That manifests into the splendid and divine.

Ideas are manufactured into inventions
Chronicled only by our willingness to succeed
Driven by our perseverance and persistence
Into a tangible art form for the whole world to embrace.

© 1998 Jan Shaw King

Expression Page

_____
_____
_____
_____
_____
_____
_____
_____
_____
_____
_____
_____
_____
_____
_____
_____
_____
_____
_____
_____
_____
_____
_____
_____
_____
_____
_____
_____

"Mt. Denali (formerly Mt. McKinley), Alaska"
Watercolor 21" X 28", © 2010 Jan Shaw King

THE JOURNEY OF LIFE

How rare is the sense of adventure
That wondrous curiosity that shines within.
How delightful when it thrusts its grand scheme into our lives
That awakens our slumbering universe.

Some shy away, afraid to take risks
While others advance boldly with abandon
Facing danger with prepared knowledge
Tackling the challenges that lurk in the shadows.

What a proud achievement
To champion through adversity
And strengthen our resolve
Toward a meaningful testament of Life.

© 1998 Jan Shaw King

Expression Page

_____
_____
_____
_____
_____
_____
_____
_____
_____
_____
_____
_____
_____
_____
_____
_____
_____
_____
_____
_____
_____
_____
_____
_____
_____
_____

FORGIVENESS

Forgiveness comes hard
When we have been abandoned
When our lives have been sucked out of our skin
When we no longer feel the warmth
Of the sun radiating our hearts.

Forgiveness comes hard
When we have been abused
And love has failed us
When our sense of wholeness
And trust have been shattered.

But like the butterfly
Who sleeps peacefully in its cocoon
Through fierce wind and pelting rain,
Love awakens to the warmth of the sun
As it unfurls its golden wings.

Over time,
Sadness and pain transform into understanding
Draping a cloak of forgiveness
That bathes us in moonlight
And warms the coldest of hearts.

The golden sun rises in radiant splendor
And Love enters once more.

Expression Page

_____
_____
_____
_____
_____
_____
_____
_____
_____
_____
_____
_____
_____
_____
_____
_____
_____
_____
_____
_____
_____
_____
_____
_____
_____
_____

"Pigeon Point Light, CA"
Watercolor 22" x 15", © 1998 Jan Shaw King

After moving to California, needing a connection from East Coast to West Coast, while recovering from Cancer, the Lighthouse became my beacon of Hope. I painted a series of Lighthouses, named my art studio: Beacons of Light, and designed/developed a Website of Lighthouses throughout the United States.

Expression Page

I AM THE LIGHT*

I am the Light.
I am Love.
I am the Truth.
I am the Power within.
I am with you always.
You have nothing to fear.

I surround you with My love.
You will radiate your love through Me
And bring your gift of love to others through your soul.

Love radiated through me when I held my hands up.
I felt pressure, struggled and fought.
I didn't believe it at first. I closed my eyes and centered.
I am in touch with my internal Self
External no longer exists.

Energy pressed against my hands.
A flooding of warmth radiated through me.
Electrical forces connected
As a conduit through our souls.

The white light of Peace surrounded me
And I was filled with an aura of light.
I am incredibly at peace
And we are one.

I laughed out loud
And was filled with joy that tickled my soul.
Like a shaft of light, energy surged through my contact.
My Spirit Guide connected me with another spirit
Whose energy radiated back into mine.

I transferred my energy as a gift to my "soul mate"
And transcended my purest love across many miles.
The Spirit Connector guides me and safely holds me
Then embraces us together and joins our souls.

© 1998 Jan Shaw King

I wrote this verse after attending a Reiki Circle. Later, I became a Reiki Practitioner.

Expression Page

_____
_____
_____
_____
_____
_____
_____
_____
_____
_____
_____
_____
_____
_____
_____
_____
_____
_____
_____
_____
_____
_____
_____
_____
_____

BLIND FAITH*

Oh, beautiful Spirit
Who guides me
Holding my hand through uncertainty,
Walking close beside me, leading the way
Through a dark and mysterious void
You embrace me.

Our souls join on our journey
Trusting, confident
That together we will meet any challenge.
You offer up my senses to enlighten my soul
A refreshing gift that
Breathes through me.

Oh, gentle Spirit
I am so grateful
For showing me that I do not need to struggle alone,
To reach out and hold your hand when I stumble,
To secure my footing,
And take one step at a time.

For this I am truly grateful
And I am blessed.

© 1998 Jan Shaw King

*I wrote this verse after Healing Odyssey's Blind Faith exercise, blindfolded, guided by a sighted partner, then switched roles with complete trust.

Expression Page

_____
_____
_____
_____
_____
_____
_____
_____
_____
_____
_____
_____
_____
_____
_____
_____
_____
_____
_____
_____
_____
_____
_____
_____
_____
_____
_____
_____

ONE STEP UP AT A TIME*

When I am out of control
And careen into a tailspin
And I feel lost and alone,
I pull up on the throttle, out of the nosedive
And glide onto an even plateau.

When I am heading for rocks
That threatens my soul
And all that makes me whole,
Take a different tact and put wind in my sails
That will guide me safely back home.

When I plunge over waterfalls
In the whirlpools of life
Swallowed up by rivers unknown,
I paddle with strength, hope and courage
And steer safely back to shore.

When surging through rapids
Angling rocks and boulders
And my fear begins to take hold
I put on my life vest and maintain my balance
With strength on my own course once more.

When I leap into the unknown with fearless abandon
To the spikes and thorns down below,
I release my parachute that guides me to safety
Where serenity will make me whole.

I strap on my harness
When life overwhelms me,
I lean over jagged rocks below,
I climb into my life full of magic and splendor

And take One Step UP at a Time.   © 1998 Jan Shaw King

*I wrote this verse when I was feeling empty, broken apart, and frustrated from being extremely ill while being treated with radiation. It seemed like an unending journey stretched out in front of me. A friend reminded me to take "One Step UP at a Time", each moment, each day, take deep breaths, and look ahead with positive thoughts, and imagine a peaceful place of serenity. Good Life Skills: I continue to practice Mindfulness every day.

Expression Page

_____
_____
_____
_____
_____
_____
_____
_____
_____
_____
_____
_____
_____
_____
_____
_____
_____
_____
_____
_____
_____
_____
_____
_____
_____
_____
_____
_____

HOLD ON

Hold on, 'cause there will be an answer
Hold on, it's comin' 'round the bend
Hold on, be patient while you're waiting
Everything will turn out in the end.

There's been too much darkness
A void that swallowed me
When there was nowhere left for me to turn
All my hope was dyin' 'till you came into my life
Now I see the light that's shining bright.

All my life I've struggled, trying hard to please
For others who never cared for me
It's hard for me to imagine my life will turn around
But you came and said these loving words to me:

Hold on, 'cause there will be an answer
Hold on, it's comin' 'round the bend
Hold on, be patient while you're waiting
Everything will turn out in the end.

You say that you've been working hard
You say your 'fridge is pretty lean
Everythin' you're doin' will build on your own
And soon you'll have a happy home.

Hold on, 'cause there will be an answer
Hold on, it's comin' 'round the bend
Hold on, be patient while you're waiting
Everything will turn out in the end.

© 1998 Jan Shaw King

Expression Page

_____
_____
_____
_____
_____
_____
_____
_____
_____
_____
_____
_____
_____
_____
_____
_____
_____
_____
_____
_____
_____
_____
_____
_____
_____
_____

LOVE THYSELF

I told myself "I love you"
Before I went to bed last night.
I kissed myself and hugged myself
And tucked myself in.

It felt strange.
And it felt good.
I felt loved.
I am loved.

I am whole.
I am one with the Universe.
I am God's wonder child.
I am special.

I am my very best friend.

Expression Page

_____
_____
_____
_____
_____
_____
_____
_____
_____
_____
_____
_____
_____
_____
_____
_____
_____
_____
_____
_____
_____
_____
_____
_____
_____

THE WARRIOR*

Even a warrior, strong of spirit and sharp of will,
Has moments that challenge the soul.

It is not the stumble that defines the greatness
Of a warrior's resolution.

It is how she stands in the face of the gale,

How she plants her feet in that moment and says,
"I fear, but I will not relent.

I will stand fast and will not erode.

I, a warrior strong, may mix my tears
With the torrent of rain that beats against me.

But I will <u>not</u> fall to the gale.

© 2015 Jim King

*Extra special thanks to my wonderful husband for his loving support and encouragement. He wrote this verse when I had learned that I had developed cardiac issues. I had to face serious medical procedures, which can be difficult since I suffer from Medical PTSD from my battle with cancer.

He wrote this verse to remind me, in that moment, how strong I really am. He often calls me, "Wonder Woman" . . . but - he is <u>my</u> Superhero!

Expression Page

_____
_____
_____
_____
_____
_____
_____
_____
_____
_____
_____
_____
_____
_____
_____
_____
_____
_____
_____
_____
_____
_____
_____
_____
_____

"Cape Ann Light, Rockport, MA"
First Place Blue Ribbon Award
22" x 30" Watercolor, © 1993 Jan Shaw King

While taking a Master Watercolor Workshop under Martin R. Ahearn, AWS, I sat on a large rock perched far away from shore, in low tide, to paint Cape Ann Light, *en plein air,* from that vantage point. While painting, winds suddenly picked up and dark clouds arose behind the lighthouse where a storm was brewing. I captured a daring photographer perched on the rocks, taking a picture of the lighthouse in the howling wind. I became so immersed in my work that I didn't realize what was happening around me. Fellow painters on shore yelled, waved their arms at me, and pointed for me to look down. The tide was coming in, and the water quickly rose around me. The rock I was sitting on became an island surrounded by swirling, angry currents of the ocean. The only way for me to save my watercolor painting was to slide down the rock, hold my painting tight, high above me, so it wouldn't get wet, which acted like a sail in the strong wind. Water rose shoulder deep, while my bare feet tentatively navigated unseen rocks below in the deep water. I safely made it to shore and looked back where I was sitting on the rock. The rock had completely disappeared below the surface of the water. Above, is the painting I nearly drowned to save. What an adventure!

*This experience became an analogy of what I was to face in the future.

Expression Page

_____
_____
_____
_____
_____
_____
_____
_____
_____
_____
_____
_____
_____
_____
_____
_____
_____
_____
_____
_____
_____
_____
_____
_____
_____

THE MEANING OF LIFE

I know the true meaning of Life
That life is too precious to waste
That love is ours to give
And all the little frustrations in life do not matter.

Only our existence has meaning
To pave a path for others to follow
With courage and dignity
Through sadness and pain
Until we reach joyful bliss
On the other side of our journey.

And this much I know,
We are never alone.

We may walk our path alone and feel lonely.
But I guarantee, we are absolutely never alone.
The Lord is always with you.
And there is always someone ~

    ... Who will reach out and hold your hand,
    ... To guide you, comfort you, console you,
    ... Listen to you, hug you, love you

And bring you peace.

And when we come out on the other side,
It is our privilege to be there for others ~

    ...To reach out, hold their hand,
    ...Guide them, comfort them, console them,
    ...Listen to them, hug them, love them

And share our Peace.

I embrace Life and each brand, new day
To begin this journey again!

© 1998 Jan Shaw King

Expression Page

SECOND CHANCE

I know a secret that I wish everyone could know
That life is beautiful and rich as a tapestry
Woven with the one thing that matters the most
That we are here to love one another
And to be loved in return.

When I had cancer, I faced death I had feared with dread.
Although I am not anxious to meet death again
I know that when my time comes,
I will not be afraid because I will have fulfilled my destiny,
My true purpose for being, and I will be next to God's side.

I have survived cancer and I have a second chance on life.
My journey is a path that I would not have readily chosen
But my voyage has taught me well
The true meaning of Life
Filled with magic and wonder.

Love is the answer. Loving and giving to one another,
Standing together when the road is hard,
Holding each other's hand and
Hugging each other through the struggle
And forgiving those who are afraid and don't understand.

My experience is not unique, yet it's uniquely mine.
My struggle pales in comparison to others,
Yet my suffering was my lonely battle to overcome.
And I have been well-rewarded,
Celebrating the little joys that come in fleeting moments!

It's my turn to reach out to hold someone else's hand
To support and guide their journey toward recovery.

© 1997 Jan Shaw King

Expression Page

_____
_____
_____
_____
_____
_____
_____
_____
_____
_____
_____
_____
_____
_____
_____
_____
_____
_____
_____
_____
_____
_____
_____
_____
_____

SOMEONE ELSE

"You have Cancer!"
I'll never forget those words.
And what an impact they had on me when I heard them.
What is most important is how I dealt with those words,
And what to do with the outcome.

I can't believe this happened to me.
These things only happen to "Someone Else."
The 6 o'clock news is filled with "Someone Else."
The newspaper headlines and obituaries are about "Someone Else."
Fund-raisers for life-threatening diseases are for "Someone Else."
Now that "Someone Else" is me. It's my turn.

Why am I playing this role?
Why was I chosen?
I cannot possibly fit the part.
I did not audition for this.
But I won the lottery.
The ticket had my name on it.

As I go through this process, feelings of fear overcome me.
Gratitude for having been spared overwhelms me.
The word, "Cancer" conjures up fear.
Everyone says I am so brave. I don't feel brave.
I only know that it is important to face what is dished out to me.
It is how I handle the situation,
How I maneuver through the turbulent times,
And how I come out of it as a true survivor.

It is most important that we support each other along the way.
The outpouring of friendship and kindness,
The tremendous amount of support
That I've been given in this strange new role that has held me up,
And gave me life support.
To my family and all my old and new friends,
I am truly grateful.

The fight is not over yet.
I will take each step at a time.
There have been major advancements in cancer research.
And I will be one of the lucky survivors. I know I will be fine.

Expression Page

_____
_____
_____
_____
_____
_____
_____
_____
_____
_____
_____
_____
_____
_____
_____
_____
_____
_____
_____
_____
_____
_____
_____
_____
_____

SOMEONE ELSE *(continued)*

In spite of this test that I have been put through, I will prevail!
I will continue to carry on and accomplish great things
And fulfill my purpose.

I now have a better understanding of others who deal
With life-threatening circumstances on a daily basis,
The infected who fight the fight,
And ranks of warriors who battle the diseases,
Dedicated surgeons, doctors, nurses, and radiologists.
They are the real heroes.
I have only recently been given a taste
Of this miracle of being reborn, my rebirth of life.
While "Someone Else" continues to struggle to survive.

Holding this ticket has included me in a club
That I never wanted to join.
But it has made me a stronger person,
Baring my soul wide open to new challenges.
I am determined to make a difference.
It has introduced me to people I hadn't known before,
Shown me a compassionate side of human nature
That I had almost forgotten.
It has brought me closer to those I love
In ways I would never have expected.

It is important never to forget everyone's kindness.
And it is important that we give back and support others.
I will carry on, produce entertainment that will heal
"Someone Else," bring happiness and joy to others,
Write and create art that will make a difference.
I walked through the fire and emerged stronger.
I am one of the lucky ones. And I am so thankful.
We must never forget that there is always..."Someone Else."

"Someone Else" became me.
I am "Someone Else."
And whatever my journey, I stand ready.
And together, my friend,
We will not only survive, but thrive
To achieve great things!

© 1997 Jan Shaw King

Expression Page

IT'S NOT TOO LATE

Stop abusing yourself.
Love yourself.
Take good care of yourself.
Give yourself your Life.

Parent yourself.
Take care of your spirit, mind, body, lungs and heart.
Exercise. Get enough rest. Eat healthy foods.
Do not add fat to your body.

Maintain your body like a well-run machine.
The human body is an incredible organ.
Your mind is an incredible organ.
You control your mind.
Do not allow your mind, or other people to control you.

At times you feed negative thoughts into your mind.
Change your thought process.
Feed positive thoughts into your mind.
You control your thoughts and actions.
You can take charge of your life and change your life.
You have the power to do anything.

Stop overeating.
Get enough rest and exercise.
Stop making excuses and just do it.
Take care of your lungs and your heart.

Give your body a treat.
Give your body a luxurious bath or lathering in the shower.
Give yourself a massage after a long, hard day at work.
Love your body outside.
And love your body inside at the same time.
Feed your body nourishing foods and thoughts.

It is all about choices.
It is all about who you are and what you want for yourself.
Nurture your talents and release your creative soul.
Love others. Give back. Forgive yourself.
"Do unto others as you would have others do unto you!"

Be your best friend. Take care of yourself first.
You must want only the best for yourself.
You must love yourself that much.
Then help someone else.   © 1998 Jan Shaw King

Expression Page

_____
_____
_____
_____
_____
_____
_____
_____
_____
_____
_____
_____
_____
_____
_____
_____
_____
_____
_____
_____
_____
_____
_____
_____
_____

"Point Vicente Light at Sunset, CA"
15" x 22" Watercolor, © 2002 Jan Shaw King

Friends took me to Point Vicente Light on the CA rocky coast to see the view from this vantage point at Sunset, which inspired me to paint the majesty of this scene.

SURVIVING AND RECOVERING

Repeat this daily:

*"I am lucky. I have beat Cancer
I am a testament of survival."*

I struggle to keep my life in balance.
I struggle every day to gain back my life and hold onto it.
I am re-discovering myself.
I am re-inventing myself.
I am learning to love myself better.
I am learning to live life better than I did before.
I am teaching myself to love myself better.
I am teaching myself a better way to balance the
...physical, emotional, mental, and spiritual parts of myself.

I am in process.

Therefore, I am.   © 1998 Jan Shaw King

Expression Page

_____
_____
_____
_____
_____
_____
_____
_____
_____
_____
_____
_____
_____
_____
_____
_____
_____
_____
_____
_____
_____
_____
_____
_____

MY THANKSGIVING PRAYER

Thanksgiving...a day set aside each year for Americans to give thanks, to realize the many blessings we have that enrich our lives. Saying "Thank You" is a great thing.

And this is my Prayer:

Thank You, dear Lord, for giving my Life to me.

Facing life's challenges is sometimes difficult. But I am extremely grateful to have challenges, to earn my living. To be self-sufficient is so important. And to have my health and insurance so I can have the tests I need to remain healthy. And in spite of life's challenges, I am extremely grateful for having enthusiasm, passion, compassion, a sense of humor, humility, talent, perseverance, and an abundant amount of faith. I pray for more patience and understanding. I never have enough.

Thank You, Lord, for this glorious, sunny day. And thank you for making me complete so I can see wonderful things around me, flowers, trees and blue sky, hear the glorious sound of chirping birds, barking dogs, waves of the ocean. To have a voice to say "I Love You" to those precious to me. To be able to walk, to write this prayer, to think, to remember, to be blessed with my wonderful family and friends.

Thank you for giving me talents that I can share with others. Painting is truly a passionate gift that comes from my soul. Thank you for guiding me and showing me the way when life gets hard. It's nice to know I am never alone when it gets lonely. I'm so grateful for having a home, a place I can come home to, and shelter from storms. Even though I want to improve my lifestyle, I am fortunate for what I have. I love my little treasures, my car that takes me safely to and from, my squishy pillows when I go to sleep at night, my warm, comfy comforter when nights get cold, having a bath and shower that's luxurious every day. Even though the cupboard is sometimes bare, somehow You provide, and I never go hungry.

Thank you, for blessing me with my beautiful children and grandchildren, the pride of my life, and how miraculous they are. I pray for them every day that you will watch over them, keep them safe, guide them, and help them find their way, with compassion, love and understanding. And most of all, for my dear, wonderful husband, my closest friend who honors me and cherishes me, as I cherish him and his loving friendship, who provides wise counsel during good times and bad.

As I look ahead to a successful future, I hope that I will never lose this sense of wonder and humble appreciation of how fortunate I am, and the love I have been given. For that is the one thing that I am thankful for, most of all. Now I want to pay it forward. Thank you, Lord, for these gifts and your Almighty blessing.

~ © 2024 Jan Shaw King

Expression Page

_____

_____

_____

_____

_____

_____

_____

_____

_____

_____

_____

_____

_____

_____

_____

_____

_____

_____

_____

_____

_____

_____

_____

_____

_____

_____

"Pigeon Point Light, CA with Shells"
Watercolor 20" x 14", © 2002 Jan Shaw King

I designed a graphic poster to promote my Lighthouse Watercolor Painting Workshops. I grew up with Lighthouses, and they have always been symbolic as a Beacon of Hope, Strength, and Courage.

Expression Page

_____
_____
_____
_____
_____
_____
_____
_____
_____
_____
_____
_____
_____
_____
_____
_____
_____
_____
_____
_____
_____
_____
_____
_____
_____
_____
_____

ORIGINAL QUOTE

"In Life's toughest moments,

An Angel appears...

God sent you."

LIST OF ORIGINAL WATERCOLOR IMAGES
BY JAN SHAW KING

For additional copies of this book, please contact:

Jan Shaw King
WBDigitalPress@gmail.com
www.WyldBlueDigitalPress.com

For more information about the Author-Illustrator,
and to purchase high-quality prints of the artwork,
please check out these Web sites:

www.JanShawKing.com
www.SeaTurtleRock.com

imprint of WBE Global LLC

ACKNOWLEDGMENTS

LIFE LINES: Verses for Reflection and Recovery has been an amazing journey. It's impossible to thank everyone who has been kind and supportive throughout the last 27 years since I was diagnosed with uterine and ovarian cancer. Writing this book, compiling verses, and marrying them with my watercolor illustrations, is a labor of love.

Heroes and Mentors

Donna Farris, Founder/President, Healing Odyssey – who encouraged me to continue to publish my book, *LIFE LINES: Verses for Reflection and Recovery*, an avid supporter, who, with her Healing Odyssey team 26-years ago, taught me how to pick up the pieces, learn new life skills, and reinvent myself.

"Grandma Angel" Alma Langill – my first art teacher since I could pick up a crayon, who taught me how to "see" the world around me, nature, colors, shadows, shapes, light, darks, and how they interact with each other, use of pastels and crayons, how to shade and combine to create new colors. This is how I "see" and imagine when I write, also.

Legendary Illustrator, Eloise Wilkin – who, after meeting at her book signing, invited me to her home for lunch to discuss and share her children's book illustrations, and to encourage me to continue illustrating my charming characters, writing and storytelling, and who introduced me to an Editor at Golden.

Martin R. Ahearn, AWS, American Watercolorist, Watercolor painter and instructor of watercolor workshops – who taught me how to "see" light sources and changing colors in nature, how to capture that moment in time, to create excitement and/or serenity in my work, to use simple strokes to tell a story, to envision and imagine more than what is real. This is how I write, also.

5th Grade teacher, Mrs. Quackenbush (the best teacher-name ever) - who praised me for my drawings and stories. She was a fan of Eloise Wilkin, also. I discovered her letter to Eloise that she saved in Eloise's scrapbook when we had lunch.

6th Grade teacher, Mrs. Weaver – who encouraged me to write stories that I knew, from my heart. Due to her kind encouragement, I was able to write what I imagined.

Mrs. Mann, Girl Scout Leader – who encouraged a deeper connection to nature and taught me basic survival skills with patience and kindness.

Wayne Williams, Art Professor/Sculptor – who praised my illustrating, drawing, painting, and sculpting skills, who gently corrected, guided my techniques, and encouraged my creativity.

Dr. David Kline, M.D., and Dr. Ronald Leuchter, M.D., Oncology Specialist – who saved my life after cancer surgeries and radiation treatments, who told me that I would be "cancer free" in 2 years, giving me hope, and something to envision and hold onto.

Dr. Wayne Dees, Neuropsychologist, Screenwriter, Producer – who drove me to the hospital for my cancer surgeries; brought food to me for my first two weeks after surgery; took me to a Dodgers game at Dodgers Stadium; visited Old Point Loma Lighthouse, San Diego; and took me to the lighting of the Hollywood Sign for the 2000 Millennium celebration.

Scott Moyer, Songwriter, Composer - Special thanks for his friendship, introducing me to Meditation Mount, Ojai, CA for meditation and healing, his music, gigs at Café Cordiale, and visiting during my recovery.

Dr. Wayne Dyer, self-help author, motivational speaker – whom I met at the Governor's Conference in CA, encouraged me to continue to follow my dreams by setting goals and following through, to never give up.

Dr. Deepok Vivek, Cardiologist; Dr. Luis Garcia, Electrophysiologist – who saved my life from cardiac complications during the last few years.

Kathy Radocaj, R.N., Lead Pediatric Oncology Nurse, Los Angeles Children's Hospital (ret.), my neighbor in California – who encouraged me to heal; took me to Reiki sessions; who fought her own battle from cancer years later – a true survivor!

Karen Miller, Executive VP, Spelling Entertainment - who came to visit me after my first surgery, took me to her home to recover for a week. Los Angeles is truly the City of Angels.

Bonnye Rosen, Producer, Writer – who shared the best breakfasts on Santa Monica Beach, and our quests to write, produce and pitch scripts and screenplays, for major studios. Courageous cancer survivor!

Tim Trombitas, Pastor, Radio, Children's TV Series Host, Producer – who hired me to write/illustrate the kids newsletter for his children's TV show, which launched me toward a new career in television and film as Writer, Screenwriter, Producer and Director of TV Series and film. He taught me to be tough, resourceful, and resilient.

Lynn Allmandinger, Matron of Honor, Insurance agent, Themed Entertainment, my "Nutcracker sister," (collectors of Nutcrackers) – who unfailingly encourages me, supports my writing and painting, and has been with me through thick and thin.

Dr. Kerry Szymanski, Daughter, Director Women's Business Center, Marketing, Entrepreneur, Speaker, and Stand-up Comedian - who inspires me with her kindness, determination to become successful, and dedication toward helping others.

Dusty Szymanski Sylvanson, Son, Mindfulness Teacher, Wilderness Survival Instructor, Master Carpenter of Strawbale homes – who taught Mindfulness to me; taught wilderness survival techniques to me before my wilderness trip to Alaska; horseback riding up a mountain in Colorado, months prior to my cancer diagnosis; for bringing me home from Cedar Sinai hospital post-surgery, to care for me a few days; and for sharing outdoor adventures; and for bringing me to beautiful scenic landscapes to paint in Colorado.

Jason Szymanski, Son, Professor of Earth Sciences, Geology and Astronomy – who came to visit soon after my surgeries and radiation for support; who writes stories, novels and attends Writer Groups; for sharing our many discussions about writing, geology, archeology, outdoor adventures, astronomy, and rocket launches.

Jim King, my Husband, Writer, Storyteller, Artist, my biggest supporter, soul mate, best friend, editor, cheerleader, and collaborator – who, when I read some of my verses to him, encouraged me to release them from my computer and publish, *LIFE LINES: Verses of Reflection and Recovery* book – "They need to be published and shared with the world! It's time." Thank you, Jim, for all of your support.

Please consider joining:

HEAL IT FORWARD
INITIATIVE

In an effort to bring the power of this book to those who may benefit from it, but may not be aware of it, or unable to afford it, please consider buying a book for yourself, and buying a second book for a Friend, Family Member, Co-Worker, or acquaintance.

Unfortunately, catastrophic illness and life shattering circumstances are far too prevalent in our lives. We all know someone who has a circumstance that has upended their lives. Handing them this book could be just the helpful starting point to unlock their ability to reflect and focus their thoughts on a powerful journey toward healing their Mind, Body, and Spirit.

Helping someone find a way through the challenges of life, to start building back the shattered existence they may find themselves in, to a brighter, hope-filled life of beauty and true joy, is one of the greatest gifts you can give. I am a personal witness to the power of a single kind gesture for another being, the catalyst to my recovery and success.

Thank you for your consideration.

~ Jan Shaw King

Dear Reader,

Now that you have enjoyed my book, it would mean the world to me if you would leave your honest thoughts about this book on Amazon.com and Books2Go.com, or your preferred retailer.

This will greatly help to bring this book to others.

Thank you from the bottom of my heart –

Go forth! Live your Life!

Be blessed with good health,

Namaste

　　　~ Jan Shaw King

Additional websites to Review this book below:

www.amazon.com

www.books2read.com

www.barnesandnoble.com

www.kobo.com

Take the next step...

COMING SOON!

THE COMPANION WORKBOOK
LIFE LINES:
METAMORPHOSIS OF CHANGE
GUIDELINES FOR RECOVERY

An ancillary workbook to *LIFE LINES: Verses for Reflection and Recovery* will help guide you through your inner personal journey.
Sign up for the newsletter and look for the release date
www.WyldBlueDigitalPress.com

MORE BOOKS BY JAN SHAW KING

If you enjoyed this work by Author-Illustrator, Jan Shaw King, be sure to look for the following titles coming soon:

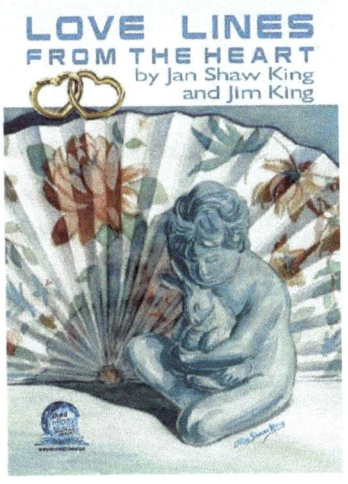

LOVE LINES FROM THE HEART

Loving, endearing collection of romantic Verses from the hearts of Jan Shaw King and Jim King, featuring endearing, heart-warming original watercolor illustrations by award-winning Watercolorist, Jan Shaw King.

NATURAL ETCHINGS

Inspirational Verses of Nature complimented by Jan Shaw King's picturesque acrylic and watercolor paintings of scenic National Parks, landscapes, and breathtaking seascapes.

Sign up for our Newsletter for all the upcoming release dates at:
www.WyldBlueDigitalPress.com

imprint of WBE Global LLC

The Israel Bible Book of Ruth
First Edition 2023
The Israel Bible was produced by Israel365 in cooperation with Teach for Israel and
is used with permission from Teach for Israel. All rights reserved.
The English translation for The Israel Bible Book of Ruth was written by Rabbi
Mordechai Gershon. All rights reserved.
Cover design and typesetting: Chani Gordon
ISBN 978-1-957-10946-6, softcover

Table of Contents

The Family Tree of King David

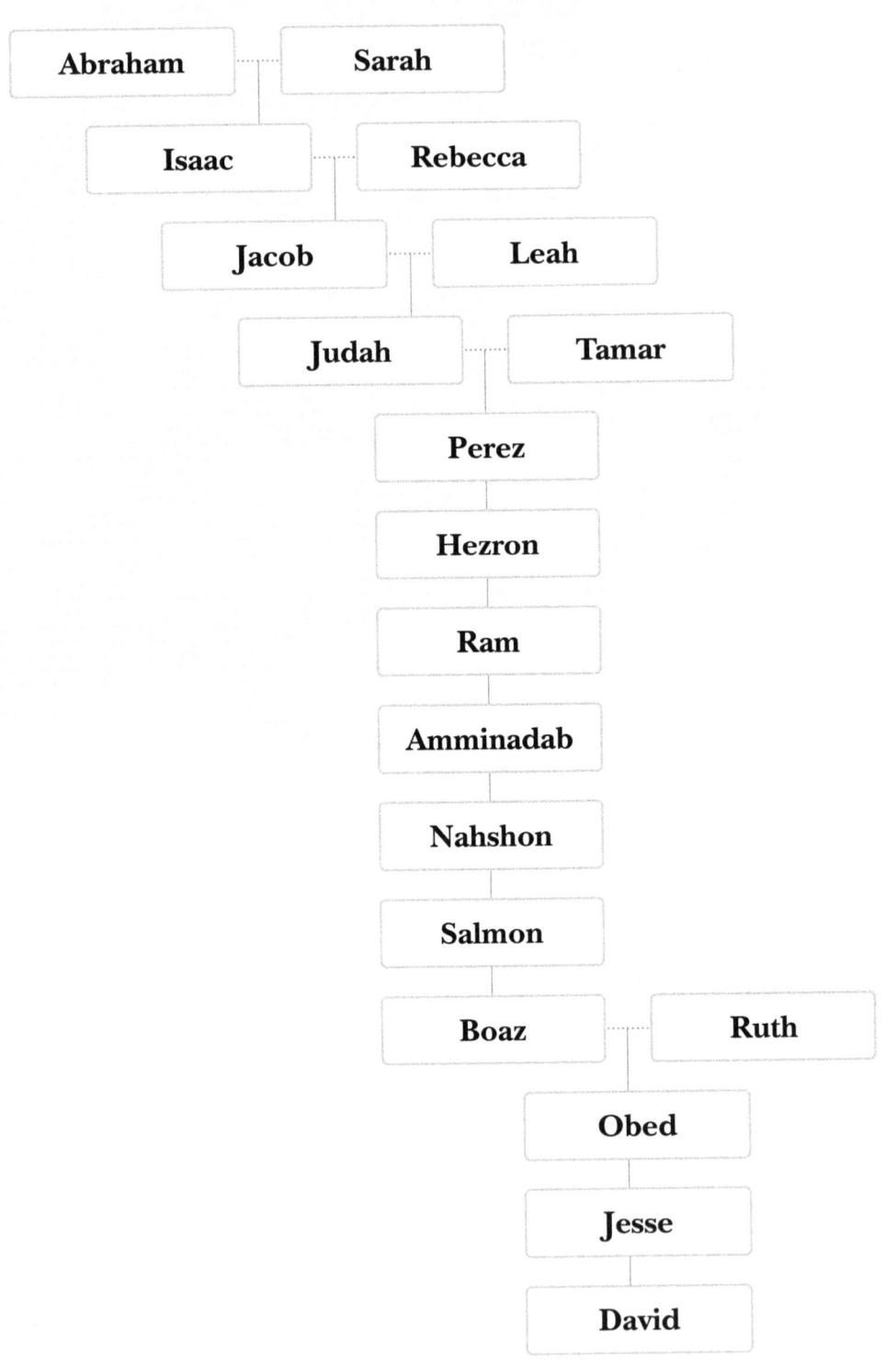

The Family Tree of Abraham & Lot

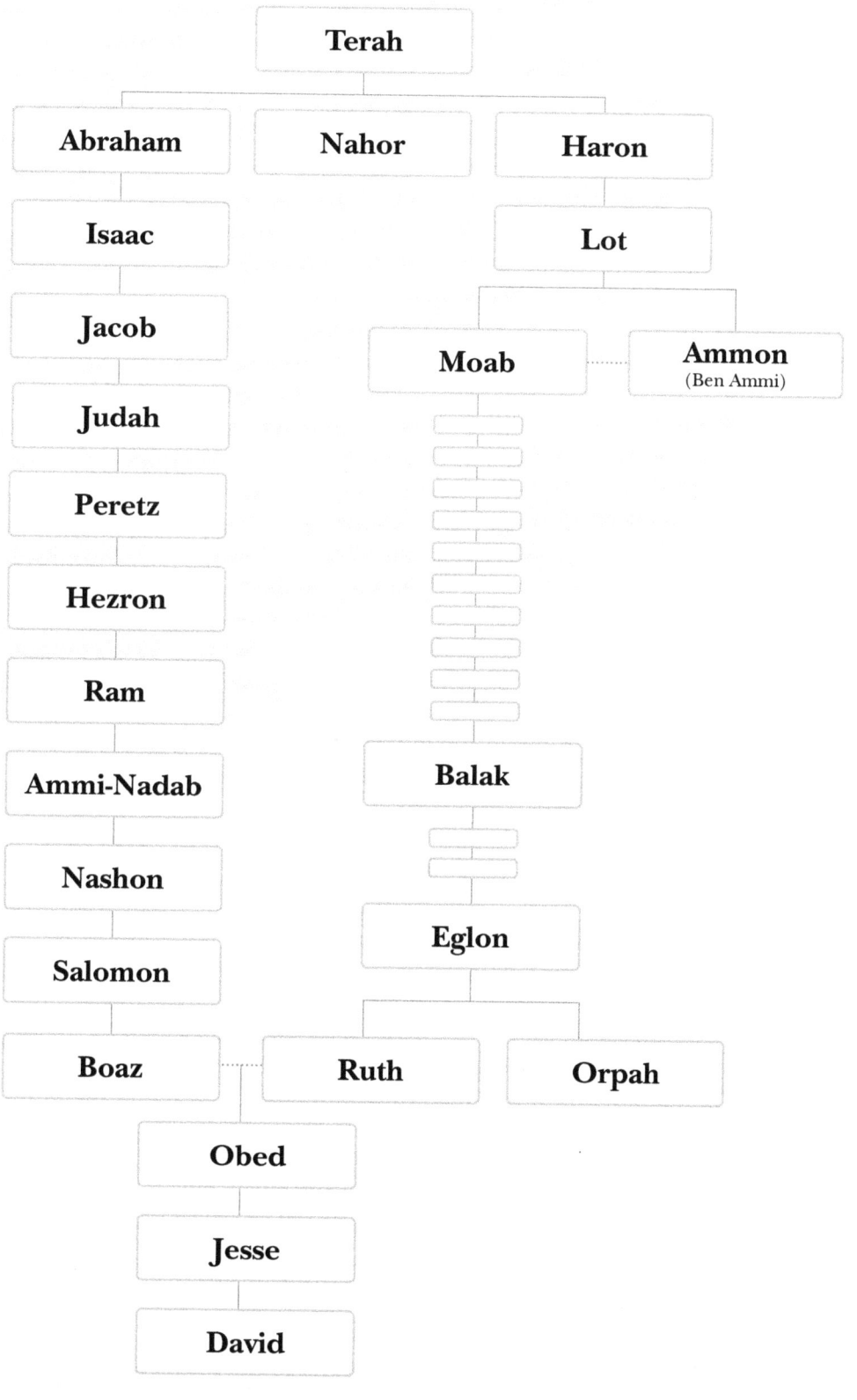

The Family Tree of
Boaz & Elimelech

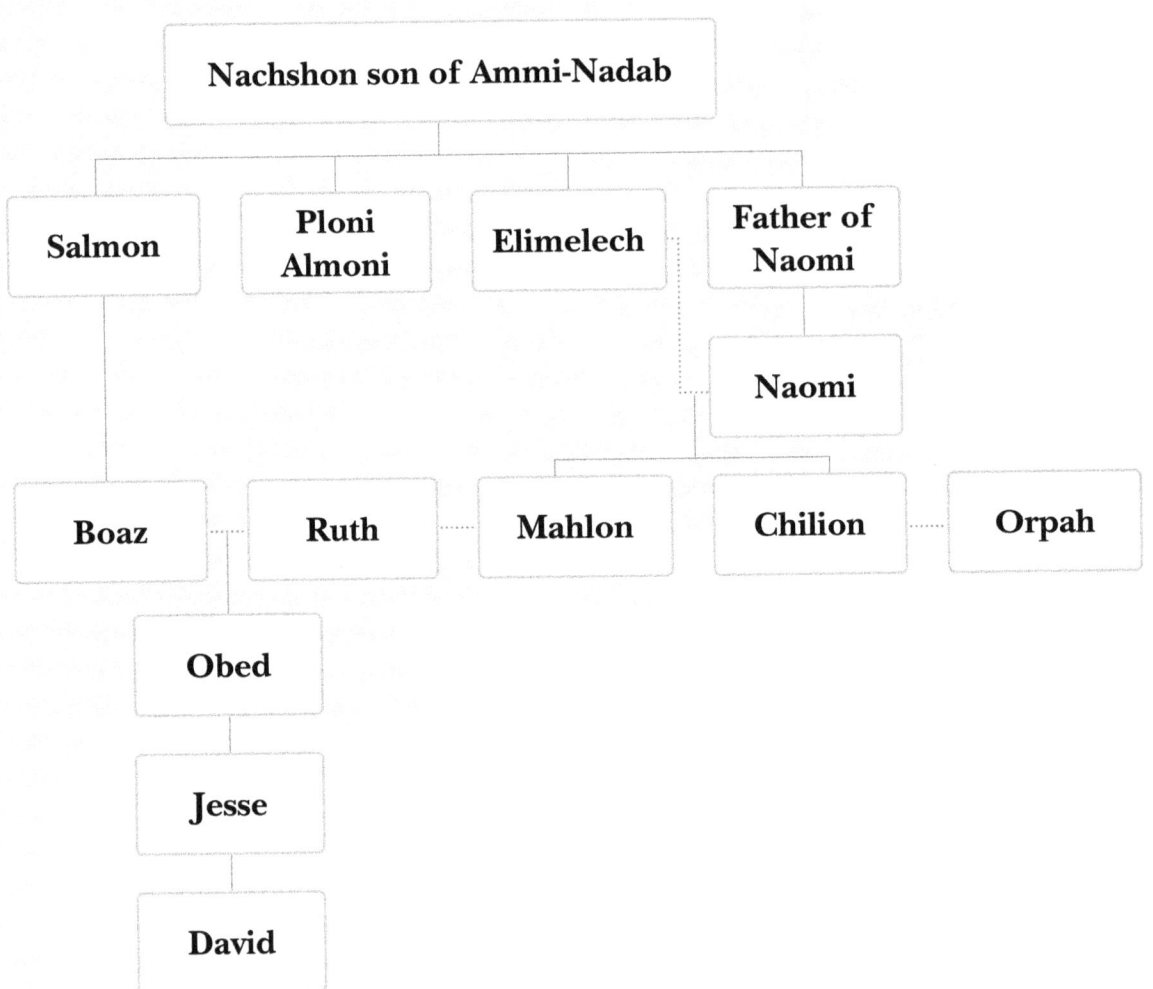

Transliterated Words

Below is a list of words that have been transliterated in the
English translation of The Israel Bible Book of Ruth:

Hebrew Name	English Name	Pronunciation	Hebrew Spelling
Aminadav	Amminadab	*a-mee-na-DAV*	עַמִּינָדָב
Beit Lechem	Bethlehem	*bayt LE-khem*	בֵּית לֶחֶם
Boaz	Boaz	*BO-az*	בֹּעַז
Chetzron	Hezron	*khetz-RON*	חֶצְרוֹן
David	David	*da-VID*	דָּוִד
Efrat	Ephrat	*ef-RAT*	אֶפְרָתָה
Elimelech	Elimelech	*e-lee-ME-lekh*	אֱלִימֶלֶךְ
Ephah	Ephah (*a dry measurement that equals a little more than a bushel*)	*ay-FAH*	אֵיפָה
Hashem	Lord/God		
Kilyon	Chilion	*kil-YON*	כִּלְיוֹן
Leah	Leah	*lay-AH*	לֵאָה
Machlon	Mahlon	*makh-LON*	מַחְלוֹן
Mara	Mara (i.e. Bitterness)	*ma-RA*	מָרָא
Nachshon	Nahshon	*nakh-SHON*	נַחְשׁוֹן

Naomi	Naomi	*na-o-MEE*	נָעֳמִי
Orpah	Orpah	*or-PAH*	עָרְפָּה
Oved	Obed	*o-VAYD*	עוֹבֵד
Peretz	Perez	*PE-retz*	פֶּרֶץ
Ploni Almoni	So-and-so	*p'-lo-NEE al-mo-NEE*	פְּלֹנִי אַלְמֹנִי
Rachel	Rachel	*ra-KHAYL*	רָחֵל
Ram	Ram	*ram*	רָם
Rut	Ruth	*rut*	רוּת
Salma	Salmon/Salmah	*sal-MAH*	שַׂלְמָה
Shaddai	Shaddai *(often translated as "the Almighty")*	*sha-DAI*	שַׁדַּי
Tamar	Tamar	*ta-MAR*	תָּמָר
Yehuda	Judah	*y'-hu-DAH*	יְהוּדָה
Yishai	Jesse	*yi-SHAI*	יִשַׁי
Yisrael	Israel	*yis-ra-AYL*	יִשְׂרָאֵל

Ruth's Lessons for Overcoming Tragedy

By Rabbi Tuly Weisz

The people of Israel are reeling from an unremitting wave of Arab terror attacks targeting innocent men, women and children throughout the Holy Land. The Book of Ruth provides a timely perspective on how to persevere, and ultimately overcome great tragedy and suffering.

In ancient Israel, during a time of political instability and financial difficulties, Elimelech and Naomi of Judea moved their family from Bethlehem to Moab across the Jordan River. Despite their attempt to find relief from the intensity and hardship of life in Israel, things go from bad to worse. During that fateful sojourn in Moab, Elimelech died, followed shortly afterward by the death of Machlon and Kilyon, his two sons. Devastated by the death of her husband and sons, Naomi decided to return home to Israel. In utter desperation, the widow cries out to her former friends and neighbors, "Don't call me Naomi," she told them. "Call me Mara, because the Almighty has made my life very bitter. I went away full, but the Lord has brought me back empty" (1:21).

More than 3,000 years later, Israel again finds itself struggling with instability and hardship. On the second day of Passover, 2023, a British family that moved to Israel set out together on a family trip from their home in Efrat on the outskirts of Bethlehem. Rabbi Leo Dee and his wife Lucy, along with their children Keren, Rina, Tali, Maia and Yehuda were driving north through the Jordan Valley on their way to Tiberias, when a Palestinian terrorist opened fire, killing Rina, 15, and Maia, 20, on the spot. Tragically, their mother Lucy, 48, succumbed to her wounds days later.

The entire nation of Israel was devastated by this vicious Passover attack, transforming the holiday from a time of great joy to a time of brokenness and pain. No one could look at the pictures of these three beautiful and holy young women, robbed of their futures, without breaking into tears. That Rina and Maia were the third set of Jewish siblings murdered by Palestinian terrorists in the course of a few weeks was simply unbearable. We all held our breath and prayed nonstop for Lucy to recover, and when she, too, died from her injuries, it seemed like all was lost. How would we ever recover from such a tragedy?

So many young friends of the Dee family filled the funeral home in Gush Etzion and the sobbing of hundreds of teenagers pierced the hearts of people all over the world. We were all shattered and broken as we gathered to listen to Rabbi Leo Dee eulogize his wife and daughters. We braced ourselves for what he had to say, expecting Rabbi Leo to cry out like Naomi, "I went away full, but the Lord has brought me back empty!"

Rabbi Dee, however, said almost the exact opposite of Naomi's words. Rather than cry out for his loved ones, he focused his attention, and ours, on faith in God, and in doing so taught the world a great lesson. "There is one main formula for faith: always focus on what you do have and not on what you do not," he said in his powerful, epic eulogy for his daughters.

At the funerals and throughout the week of *shiva*, Rabbi Dee found a great reservoir of inner strength to use his indescribable pain to bring something positive to the world. Rabbi Leo accepted his terrible burden with heroic courage and penetrating wisdom. At the funerals, he encouraged people to do more good. At the *shiva*, he called reporters to task for their irresponsible media bias and moral equivalency in blaming "both sides" for the endless "cycle of violence." He inspired the many thousands of friends and strangers who entered his home during the *shiva* to do something big or small to make the world a better place. He encouraged people to add an Israeli flag to their social media profile pictures and to flood the world with Israeli pride.

Almost immediately, people all over the world launched meaningful projects in memory of Lucy, Maia and Rina. Within days, more than ten thousand people signed up to study the Ethics of our Fathers, and countless others joined together to recite Psalms. Rabbi Dee and his family launched three ambitious projects in the Efrat community in memory of his wife and two daughters.

The Lucy Dee Simcha Hall will be an exquisite event hall to celebrate community and life events, honoring Lucy's joyful disposition and her involvement in the community so near and dear to her. The Rina Dee Youth Center will be a building dedicated to the Ezra youth movement, where Rina served as a beloved youth counselor for 6th-grade girls. Maia Dee's Spring will be a park that commemorates Maia's love for nature and water. It will be embedded in a beautifully designed landscape of foliage, flowers and trees, including picnic and play areas for all ages.

This volume of the Book of Ruth, which we traditionally read on the holiday of Shavuot, is dedicated in memory of Lucy, Rina and Maia Dee and will serve as an eternal monument to their lives. As the holiday of Shavuot and the giving of the Bible on Mount Sinai complete the process of redemption that began on Passover, we pray that *The Israel Bible Book of Ruth,* and the lessons it contains for overcoming devastation and tragedy, will provide some healing and comfort on Shavuot after the devastating loss of Lucy, Maia and Rina on Passover.

In the Book of Ruth, the bereaved Naomi was initially unable to overcome her personal pain. Only through Ruth's selfless acts of love and the great kindness of Boaz, does the sad story turn into a tale of redemption. In our own day, the Dee family refused to succumb to their own personal pain and immediately initiated acts of chesed, while teaching us all never to waiver in our faith in God and our commitment to the land of Israel. May God bring comfort to Rabbi Leo, Keren, Tali and Yehuda Dee, and raise up the holy souls of Lucy, Rina and Maia, hy"d.

Rabbi Tuly Weisz
Founder of Israel365 and Publisher of The Israel Bible
Ramat Beit Shemesh, Israel
Iyar 5783 / May 2023

Introduction to Megillat Rut

By Rabbi Tuly Weisz

The Book of Ruth provides a timely perspective on overcoming tragedy and devastation for our generation that is reeling from an unremitting wave of terror attacks on Israelis.

In ancient Israel, during a time of political instability and financial difficulties, Elimelech and Naomi of Judea moved their family from Bethlehem to Moab across the Jordan River. During their attempt to find reprieve from the intensity and hardship of life in Israel, things go from bad to worse. During that fateful sojourn, Elimelech died along with his sons Machlon and Kilyon. Naomi was devastated by the loss of her husband and two sons, and so she returns home to Israel. In utter desperation, the widow cries out to her former friends and neighbors, "Don't call me Naomi," she told them. "Call me Mara, because the Almighty has made my life very bitter. I went away full, but the Lord has brought me back empty" (1:21).

More than 3,000 years later, Israel again finds itself struggling with instability and hardship. Just a few weeks ago, a family set out together from Efrat on the outskirts of Bethlehem, to enjoy the Pesach holiday, and encountered utter devastation. Rabbi Leo Dee and his wife Lucy, along with their children Keren, Rina, Tali, Maia and Yehuda were driving north through the Jordan Valley on their way to Tiberias, when a Palestinian terrorist opened fire, killing Rina, 20, and Maia, 15, on the spot. Tragically, their mother Lucy, 48, succumbed to her wounds days later.

The entire family of Israel was devastated by this viscous Passover attack and spent the rest of the holiday in a state of shock. The brutality of the murders contrasted with the photographs of the beautiful women interrupted the joy of Pesach throughout the Jewish world. That Rina and Maia were the third set of Jewish siblings killed by Palestinian terrorists in the course of a few weeks was simply unbearable. We all held our breath and prayed nonstop for Lucy to recover from her grave injuries, and when she too died from her injuries, it seemed like all was lost. How would we ever recover from such a tragedy?

13

So many young friends of the Dee family filled the funeral home in Gush Etzion and the sobbing of hundreds of teenagers pierced the hearts of people all over the world. We were all shattered and broken, as we gathered to listen to Rabbi Leo Dee eulogize his wife and daughters. We braced ourselves for what he had to say, expecting Rav Leo to cry out like Naomi, "I went away full, but the Lord has brought me back empty!"

Rabbi Dee, however, said almost the exact opposite of Naomi's words. Rather than cry out for his loved ones, he focused his attention, and ours, on Emunah, and in doing so taught the world a great lesson. "There is one main formula for faith: always focus on what you do have and not on what you do not," he said in his powerful, epic eulogy for his daughters.

At the funerals and throughout the week of Shiva, the grieving husband and father, Leo Dee found a great reservoir of inner strength to focus all the personal and collective pain into positivity. Rav Leo accepted his terrible burden with heroic courage and penetrating wisdom. At the funerals, he encouraged people to do more good. At the Shiva he called reporters to task for their irresponsible media bias and moral equivalency in blaming 'both sides' for the endless 'cycle of violence.' He inspired the many thousands of friends and strangers who entered his home for Shiva to do something big or small to make the world a better place. He encouraged people to storm social media and add an Israeli flag to their profile pictures and his words were shared and reshared.

Almost immediately, numerous Torah and Chesed projects emerged in memory of Lucy, Rina and Maia. Within days, more than ten thousand people signed up to learn Pirket Avot, and countless others joined together to say Tehillim. Friends from Efrat committed to dedicating a Simcha Hall, a park, and a youth center in their memory. This volume of Megilat Rut, in memory of Lucy, Rina and Maia Dee is but one project that emerged in the aftermath of their death to serve as an eternal monument to their lives. Just as Shavuot is linked to Pesach through the counting of the Omer, we pray that the study of *The Israel Bible Book of Ruth* and the lessons it contains for overcoming devastation and tragedy this Shavuot provides healing for the great pain we all felt over Pesach.

In Megillat Rut, the bereaved Naomi was initially unable to overcome her personal pain. Only through Ruth's selfless acts of Chesed and the great kindness of Boaz does the sad story turn into a tale of redemption. In our own day, the Dee family refused to succumb to their own personal pain, and immediately initiated acts of chesed while teaching us all never to waiver in our faith in Hashem and our commitment to Eretz Yisrael. Through all the Torah being studied and all the chesed being performed, may Hashem bring comfort to Rabbi Leo, Keren, Tali and Yehuda Dee and raise up the holy *neshamot* of Lucy, Rina and Maia, Hashem yikom daman.

Rabbi Tuly Weisz
Ramat Beit Shemesh, Israel
Nissan 5783 / May 2023

Commentary

By Rabbi Tuly Weisz

AN INTRODUCTION TO THE BOOK OF RUTH

With only four chapters, Ruth is one of the smallest books in the Hebrew Bible. But despite its diminutive size, it holds a special place in the hearts of the Jewish people. Countless scholars have written commentaries on Ruth (most of which are much longer than the text itself!), and lay people regularly cite it as their most beloved book. But why is this book so cherished? What makes this short book so unique?

Ruth and the Holiday of Shavuot

Every year, the Jewish people read the Book of Ruth on the holiday of *Shavuot* (Pentecost), which falls out towards the end of May or early June. *Shavuot* is one of the three central pilgrimage festivals, and is the day when the Jewish people experienced revelation and received the Torah from God on Mount Sinai. But why do we read the Book of Ruth - a book that appears to have no connection to the giving of the Torah on Mount Sinai - on the day we commemorate the giving of the Torah?

The giving of the Torah was the single most important moment in the history of civilization – not just for Jews, but for all of mankind. The Sages wondered why, if the Bible is so holy, it wasn't given in the Holy Land? Why was the Bible given in a desert, and not the Land of Israel? They explain that since Israel is the Jewish homeland, had the Bible been given in Jerusalem it would have belonged exclusively to the Jewish people. Therefore, God chose to transmit His moral code on a barren mountain in the ownerless desert, to emphasize that His Word is meant not only for the people of Israel but for all mankind, because His instructions are the key to human happiness.

In the Book of Ruth, the Moabite princess Ruth forges her own path to Mount Sinai through her relationship with her Jewish mother-in-law Naomi. Ruth is associated with the holiday of Shavuot because, with great self-sacrifice, she finds her way to the ultimate truth of the Torah. As she movingly declares to Naomi: "For where you go, I will go, and where you stay, I will stay. Your nation is my nation and your God is my God.

Where you will die, I will die and I will be buried there." (Ruth 1:16-17). This redemptive experience leads Ruth to join the Jewish people and accept the Bible as her own. In doing so, Ruth paved a path for the whole world to recognize God and the Torah He gave on Mount Sinai on the holiday of *Shavuot*.

Light is Born at a Time of Darkness

Though the Book of Ruth is a personal story describing tragic and heroic individuals, it is a personal story with *national* implications. The extraordinary kindness that Ruth, Boaz and Naomi show to one another leads to the union of Ruth and Boaz and, ultimately, to the birth of their great grandson: King David.

We can better appreciate the significance of this story by placing it in its proper context. The stories described in the Book of Ruth take place at the same time as the events of the Book of Judges - a dark and difficult era for the people of Israel. After the death of Joshua, the tribes of Israel each operated independently of one another. Lacking unity, the tribes were weak and vulnerable to attack from neighboring countries and plundering tribes. At the same time, without consistently strong leadership, the Israelites frequently turned away from God and worshiped the pagan gods of surrounding nations. The Book of Judges can be described as a painful cycle: the people become complacent and turn away from God; God sends foreign enemies to subjugate the people; the people cry out and God sends a savior to redeem them; finally, saved from their enemies, the people become complacent and the cycle is repeated once again.

Like the entire era of the Book of Judges, the story of Ruth is filled with disappointments. After selflessly following her mother-in-law to Judea, Ruth is rewarded with a life of poverty and no marriage prospects. When she and her mother-in-law return to Naomi's hometown of Bethlehem, the people stare at Naomi, widowed and aged, and say "Is this broken woman really Naomi?" Living on the edge of town with no means of support, Naomi calls herself "Mara," "the bitter one" - and who can blame her?

Ruth amazingly stumbles onto Boaz's farm, and he is kind to her; you can almost hear the wedding bells! But once again, Ruth is disappointed. The harvest season ends, and nothing happens. Boaz fails to act.

In a bold move, Naomi instructs Ruth to sneak into the threshing floor where Boaz is asleep. And yet, instead of a romantic scene, Boaz essentially tells Ruth: "There may be another redeemer instead of me. Wait, and let's see what happens." This other relative is given the opportunity to marry Ruth, but he turns it down - yet another moment of rejection and disappointment! It is only then, at the very end of the book, when we finally reach the moment we've been waiting for. Boaz steps up to the plate and says "I will redeem her!" And from this union, the Messiah is born.

This, it seems, is God's playbook for redemption. Like the story of Ruth and like the entire era of the Book of Judges, the path to redemption is destined to be filled with disappointments. And yet, in the very midst of the darkness of that time, the love and kindness of a handful of people brought a powerful light to the world and planted the seeds of Israel's future redemption!

The lesson of the Book of Ruth is particularly important for our generation. In many ways, the modern State of Israel is re-experiencing the era of the Book of Judges. Modern Israel is divided into "tribes" - religious and secular, Jews of Middle Eastern origin and Jews from Europe, Jews who believe the State of Israel is the harbinger of redemption and Jews who reject its religious significance altogether. At the same time, dangerous enemies like Iran and its terror proxies threaten Israel from without, while Palestinian terrorists murder as many Jews as they can within Israel. From this perspective, we are living through an era of great pain and national disappointment.

But the Book of Ruth teaches us that it is precisely during times like this that the seeds of redemption are sown. Perhaps, at this very moment of civil strife and external threats, the story of the final redeemer is being set in motion - right under our noses!

This is why the Book of Ruth is so beloved. Ruth reminds us to never give up hope - for God will never forsake His people! Take strength, for the redemption *will* come!

CHAPTER 1 - THE LAND OF KINDNESS

Though it is never explicitly discussed, the Land of Israel is front and center in the Book of Ruth. While the primary characters in this short book do not travel extensively, geography nevertheless plays a critical role in the story.

"And it was in the days when the judges judged that there was a famine in the land. A man from *Beit Lechem*, in the territory of *Yehuda*, went to live in the fields of Moab – he, his wife, and their two sons." (Ruth 1:1). The story opens with a famine in the Land of Israel which causes a man, Elimelech, to move his family from Israel to the plains of Moab.

Already in the beginning of the Bible, the Land of Israel is plagued by famine. Upon reading the first verse in the Book of Ruth, the sensitive reader is reminded of the first famine to strike the land, which is introduced with the very same words, "there was a famine in the land" (Genesis 12:10). Through this introductory phrase and setting, the Hebrew Bible connects these two stories, and we can learn much by exploring the parallels and contrasts between the Books of Ruth and Genesis.

In Genesis 12, Hashem appears for the first time to Abraham:

> *Hashem said to Abram, "Go forth from your native land and from your father's house to the land that I will show you. I will make of you a great nation, and I will bless you; I will make your name great, And you shall be a blessing. I will bless those who bless you and curse him that curses you; And all the families of the earth shall bless themselves by you."*

> *Abram went forth as Hashem had commanded him, and Lot went with him. Abram was seventy-five years old when he left Haran. Abram took his wife Sarai and his brother's son Lot, and all the wealth that they had amassed, and the persons that they had acquired in Haran; and they set out for the land of Canaan. When they arrived in the land of Canaan, Abram passed through the land as far as the site of Shechem, at the terebinth of Moreh. The Canaanites were then in the land. Hashem appeared to Abram and said, "I will assign this land to your offspring." And he built an altar there to Hashem...*

> *Then Abram journeyed by stages toward the Negeb. There was a famine in the land, and Abram went down to Egypt to sojourn there, for the famine was severe in the land. (Genesis 12:1-10)*

Abraham is called to go to Israel where he will be granted land and offspring, in order to establish a special nation that would be the source of blessing to the entire world. The twin blessings of land and offspring are repeated to Abraham several times in Genesis:

> *"Raise your eyes and look out from where you are, to the north and south, to the east and west, for I give all the land that you see to you and your offspring forever." (13:14,15)*

> *"On that day Hashem made a covenant with Abram, saying, 'to your offspring I assign this land, from the river of Egypt to the great river, the river Euphrates." (15:18)*

> *"I assign the land you sojourn in to you and your future offspring, all the land of Canaan, as an everlasting holding." (17:8)*

From this point forward, the rest of the Bible revolves around the ups and downs of the relationship between the people of Israel and the land of Israel, for transforming a family into a nation requires a homeland. At the same time, an inheritance without progeny is meaningless. Only these two together - the land and the people - can fulfill God's mission.

Yet, almost as soon as he steps foot in the Promised Land, Abraham finds that there "was a famine in the land," and he is forced to leave shortly after he arrives. Abraham chooses to go to Egypt, a land watered by the Nile and therefore less affected by a lack of rainfall and famine. Years later, Jacob would also go down with his family to Egypt as a result of famine.

The precedent of Abraham and Jacob raises a critical question. When famine strikes Bethlehem during Elimelech's generation, why does he choose to migrate to Moab, a land with a similar climate to that of Bethlehem and most likely affected by the famine as well, rather than to Egypt like Abraham and Jacob did before him? By alluding to the famine in the time of Abraham, the Book of Ruth wants us to ask: why didn't Elimelech follow the example of Abraham? Why did he choose Moab over Egypt?

To answer these questions, we must first explain who Moab was and where Moab came from. When Abraham journeys to the Promised Land, his nephew Lot goes with him (Genesis 12:4). He, too, leaves his homeland to journey to "the land that I will show you," demonstrating that he is, at least initially, united in purpose and action with Abraham. It is only once they return from Egypt that Lot separates from his righteous uncle:

> *Lot, who went with Abram, also had flocks and herds and tents, so that the land could not support them staying together; for their possessions were so great that they could not remain together. And there was quarreling between the herdsmen of Abram's cattle and those of Lot's cattle. The Canaanites and Perizzites were then dwelling in the land. Abram said to Lot, "Let there be no strife between you and me, between my herdsmen and yours, for we are kinsmen. Is not the whole land before you? Let us separate: if you go north, I will go south; and if you go south, I will go north." Lot looked about him and saw how well watered was the whole plain of the Jordan, all of it - this was before HAshem had destroyed Sodom and Gomorrah - all the way to Zoar, like the garden of Hashem, like the land of Egypt. So Lot chose for himself the whole plain of the Jordan, and Lot journeyed eastward. Thus they parted from each other; Abram remained in the land of Canaan, while Lot settled in the cities of the Plain, pitching his tents near Sodom. Now the inhabitants of Sodom were very wicked sinners against Hashem. (Genesis 13:5-13)*

Though the dispute begins with financial matters, it does not end there. By choosing to live in the evil and sinful city of Sodom, Lot makes a fateful decision that amounts to a rejection of both Abraham and God. There are immediate consequences to Lot's decision to live in such a perilous place, and he is kidnapped by enemies soon after his arrival (Genesis chapter 14). But even after Abraham rescues him, rather than recognizing his mistake and returning with Abraham to the Land of Israel, Lot remains in Sodom. Later, the sin of Sodom is so great that God decides to destroy the city, and, once again, Lot is caught in the crossfire.

Though he lives among "wicked sinners," Lot's righteous upbringing by his uncle Abraham seems to have influenced him. Abraham is a paradigm of kindness. His tent is always open to visitors and desert wanderers. He disregards his own personal discomfort following his circumcision, choosing to wait in the desert heat, hoping that he will be able to help a tired traveler (Genesis 18:1). When his guests leave, he doesn't just bid them farewell but walks with them "to see them off" (Genesis 18:16). And when God shares the news about His intent to destroy Sodom, Abraham prays for the lives of the city's inhabitants even though they are his ideological enemies (Genesis 18:17-32).

Growing up in this environment clearly made an impact on Lot. When the angels of God enter Sodom, Lot opens his home to them. Yet the townspeople demand they be able to have their way with the men. Lot's appreciation for guests and concern for their welfare, something he learned first hand from Abraham, leads to his absurd offer to "take my daughters instead" (Genesis 19:8). Though he has taken Abraham's lessons in hospitality to heart, he clearly lacks the moral compass of his righteous uncle.

Lot imparts this perverted moral compass to the next generation. Following the destruction of Sodom, Lot's daughters, in their supposedly noble desire to perpetuate their family line, concoct a plot to get their father drunk with wine and seduce him so that they both end up pregnant with his child. While the younger daughter names her son Ben-ammi (the ancestor of the Ammonites), the older daughter names her son Moab, which means 'from my father,' a reference to his incestual origins. Moab becomes an important figure throughout the Hebrew Bible, and a rival nation to the descendants of Abraham.

From these two stories, we learn of two defining Moabite traits: a perverse relationship with kindness and a lack of sexual morality. These two behaviors reappear later in the Bible when the descendants of Abraham and the descendants of Lot meet again.

The Bible describes how the promiscuous Moabite women, themselves a product of the incestuous relationship between Lot and his daughter, seduce the Israelite men in the desert (Numbers 25:1). Furthermore, the nation of Moab exhibits a lack of hospitality and kindness towards the Jewish people in the desert when they fail to greet them with bread and water on the Israelites' journey out of Egypt (Deuteronomy 23:5).

These two rival nations grow apart so much that the Bible concludes, "No Ammonite or Moabite shall enter the community of *Hashem;* none of his descendants, even in the tenth generation, shall be admitted into the congregation of *Hashem.*" (Deuteronomy 23:4-5). Even when the Bible prohibits Jews from marrying members of other nations, those restrictions are usually limited in time and scope. For example, if an Egyptian converts to Judaim, his descendants can marry born Jews after three generations. Even the Amalekites are accepted into the Jewish nation if they accept the Jewish God and convert. However, Moabites are forbidden from converting to Judaism - even after many generations! Moab, it seems, became the spiritual heirs of Sodom, where their forefather Lot chose to live and raise his family. Their stinginess and sexual immorality, so antithetical to the values of the children of Abraham, has no place in the "congregation of *Hashem.*"

With this background, Elimelech's choice to go to Moab is even more perplexing. Why would he immigrate to a land that is so incompatible with Jewish values and join a perpetual enemy of the Jewish people?

Indeed, Elimelech is criticized in Jewish tradition for his decision to leave Israel and go to Moab. A leader of his community, his abandonment of his people and his land during a difficult famine was judged a great transgression. Sure enough, Elimelech's journey to Moab ends in personal catastrophe. He dies soon after his arrival. His sons marry Moabite women, seemingly in direct violation of the Bible's prohibition. And both of his sons, Mahlon and Chilion, die in Moab as well. It is only once Naomi and Ruth return to Israel that things start to change for the better.

What did Elimelech do wrong? According to the Talmud (*Bava Batra* 91a), Elimelech was punished for abandoning the Land of Israel, and his children were punished for staying there even after their father's death. Abandoning the Land of Israel once the Jewish nation has been established there is a sin that warrants punishment. The famine in the land was not a sign to leave, but rather God's way of calling attention to the sins of the nation, as described in Deuteronomy (11:16-17). Instead of running away, Elimelech should have stayed and encouraged the people to repent. His abandonment of the Land of Israel at the beginning of the Book of Ruth proves that exile is harmful to the Jew, and that the return to the Land - and specifically to Bethlehem - provides the rehabilitation needed not only for the family, but the nation and ultimately the entire world.

But we still must wonder: why did Elimelech, a descendant of Abraham, choose Moab of all places? As descendants of Abraham, the value of kindness is built into the DNA of the Jewish people and is something that every Jew must aspire to. Yet the Sages tell us that Elimelech was motivated to leave the Land of Israel because of stinginess. Elimelech was blessed with wealth, yet he did not want to share it with the many poor people that were knocking on his door for handouts as a result of the famine. Based on what we have learned about Moab, we can now understand why Elimelech chose to go there.

Elimelech's move to Moab was triggered by stinginess and a lack of kindness towards his poor brethren. In that way, he behaved more like a descendant of Lot than a descendant of Abraham. He therefore felt comfortable in Moab, a place known for its stinginess and lack of kindness. In Moab, caring for the poor was not a communal value, and so Elimelech would not have to worry about poor people coming and begging him to sustain them.

In this way, the land of Moab stands in stark contrast to the Land of Israel. While Moab breeds selfishness and miserliness, in the Land of Israel, the land given by God to Abraham and his descendants, the value of charity is built into the very fabric of the land. Biblical law requires farmers in Israel to leave some of their produce in the fields for the poor, a commandment highlighted in the next chapter of the Book of Ruth. Furthermore, the land itself cannot tolerate immorality, and the prophets remind us time and again that corrupt behavior will lead the Jewish people to be exiled from their land.

It is for this reason that Israel was the land chosen as an inheritance for the descendants of Abraham, the paradigm of kindness. Only in the Land of Israel can the Jewish people reach their full potential.

CHAPTER 2 - CHOOSING KINDNESS

The Hebrew Bible is divided into three sections: *Torah*, the Five Books of Moses, *Nevi'im*, Prophets, and *Ketuvim*, Writings. Each section of the Bible is Divine, but they were each written with different levels of prophetic revelation.

The Five Books of Moses were written by Moses, who received the highest level of prophecy, described in the Bible as God communicating with him "face to face"

(Numbers 12:7-8). These words were dictated to Moses directly by God, and Moses recorded them word for word. The books of the Prophets contain divine prophecies communicated to the prophets by God in a dream or a trance, and written in the prophet's own words. Finally, the books of the Writings were written through divine inspiration, without direct communication from God. Since these works were not written through direct communication with God, there was some uncertainty as to which books should and should not be included in the Bible. As such, Writings were the last section of the Hebrew Bible to be canonized. It was only formally included in Hebrew Scripture in the second century CE, based on the discussions, debates and decisions of a group of sages known as the Men of the Great Assembly.

In one such discussion, Rabbi Zeira asks why the Book of Ruth was included in the canon of Hebrew Scriptures if it does not teach us any new laws: Rabbi Zeira says, "This scroll does not have anything in it concerned with impurity or purity nor what is forbidden and what is permitted. So why is it written? To teach us the greatness of the reward for acts of lovingkindness."

According to this sage, the Book of Ruth was included in the biblical canon because of its focus on loving-kindness. Kindness is a point of pride amongst the Jewish people, the hallmark of Abraham and something that every Jew must aspire to. In fact, Maimonides writes that loving-kindness is something that is built into the genetic makeup of a Jew, and if a Jew displays a lack of kindness, or cruelty, his lineage should be called into question: "Anyone who is cruel and does not exhibit compassion, we should [suspect him and attempt to] ascertain his lineage." (Maimonides, Laws of Gifts to the Poor, 10:2)

Kindness to others is the most repeated command in the Hebrew Bible. The injunction to "love the stranger" appears no less than 36 times! The message was also repeatedly hammered home by the Hebrew prophets:

> *Wash yourselves, cleanse yourselves, take your evil deeds away, out of My sight; stop doing evil. Learn to do good, seek justice, gladden the oppressed, defend the orphan, fight for the widow. (Isaiah 1:16-17)*

> *For I desire loving-kindness, not sacrifice; Obedience to God, rather than burnt offerings. (Hosea 6:6)*

> *He has told you, O man, what is good, And what Hashem requires of you: Only to do justice and to love kindness, and to walk modestly with your God. (Micah 6:8)*

Kindness is the main theme not only of the Book of Ruth, but, according to one of the greatest sages in early Jewish history, the entire Bible! Rabbi Akiva, the universally recognized leader of his generation who died in approximately 135 CE, taught that the entire Bible could be summed up with one phrase: "Love your fellow as you love yourself" (Leviticus 19:18).

On the flipside, the antithesis of kindness is repugnant to the Bible, so much so that Moab was prohibited entry into the Jewish People for their national miserliness. What is surprising about the Book of Ruth is that the lesson of kindness is taught from a most unlikely source: Ruth the Moabite.

After the family settles in Moab, Mahlon, son of Elimelech, marries Ruth. Though she is a daughter of the cruel nation of Moab, known for their miserliness and sexual misconduct, Ruth rejects the cruelty of her people. After her Judean husband, brother-in-law and father-in-law all die, and her mother-in-law Naomi is left with nothing, Ruth and her sister-in-law Orpah offer to accompany Naomi back to Judah, a wonderful gesture.

Recognizing that she had nothing to offer her daughters-in-law and that they would lead much easier lives in Moab, Naomi demurs and tells the women to return to their families. Orpah realizes that Naomi is right, kisses her mother-in-law on the cheek and stays in Moab, the clearly more logical decision. Ruth, on the other hand, for reasons that are not made explicit in the text, surprises the reader with her stubborn attachment to Naomi. "They lifted their voices and cried extensively. Orpah kissed her mother-in-law, yet *Rut* stuck with her." (Ruth 1:14).

The verse says that Ruth "clings" to her mother-in-law, using the Hebrew words *davka bah*. This Hebrew verb connotes an all encompassing connection, such as in Genesis 2:24, where the verse says that "a man *clings* to his wife." Just as in a marriage a husband and wife are so committed to one another that they put the needs of their spouse before their own, Ruth places Naomi first, even at the expense of her own self-interest. She expresses her steadfast devotion to her mother-in-law with one of the most beautiful statements of faith and allegiance in the entire Bible:

> *"Do not compel me to leave you, to turn back from following after you. For where you go, I will go, and where you stay, I will stay. Your nation is my nation and your God is my God. Where you will die, I will die and I will be buried there. May Hashem do so for me, and even more, for only death will separate between me and you"* (Ruth 1:16-17)

From these first words uttered by Ruth, we see that although she is a descendant of Lot, Ruth displays more affinity to Abraham, who himself left his family and homeland behind in order to travel to the Promised Land. Unlike Lot who chose wealth and comfort over morals and values, Ruth turns her back on a life of comfort and instead chooses something greater: a chance to join the Jewish people and to follow the Jewish God.

Ruth's words are certainly deliberate and loaded with meaning. She first identifies the People of Israel and then the God of Israel to explain her decision to leave Moab. She recognizes the dual nature of the Jews, that they are a nation as well as a religion, and she wants both.

By declaring her allegiance to God and the Jewish people, Ruth became one of a small number of righteous non-Jews in the Bible who stand out for recognizing *Hashem*. Jethro, for example, moved by what he heard about the Exodus from Egypt, went to meet up with Moses in the desert as the Israelites were camped by the mountain of God. After Moses recounts to his father-in-law all that God had done for them, Jethro rejoices and declares: "Now I know that the LORD is greater than all gods" (Exodus 18:11). Similarly, when Joshua sends two spies to scout out the Land of Israel before the Jews cross the Jordan and enter the land, they find shelter at the inn of Rahab. She, too, is impressed by everything that God has done for the Jewish people and asserts: "For Hashem your God is the only God in heaven above and on earth below" (Joshua 2:11).

Though Ruth is not the first non-Jew in the Bible to recognize the Jewish God, none of the others have been discussed with as much detail or with so much attention to their words. She is, after all, the only one that has a whole book of the Bible dedicated to her story. Ruth is special, and her powerful words of commitment to Naomi are clearly meant to teach subsequent generations, Jews and non-Jews, what it means to cast your lot with the Jewish people.

What makes Ruth so special? It is her outstanding acts of loving-kindness that make her unique, and ultimately make her worthy of being the forebear of the Davidic dynasty. Time and again she continues to display this trait of selflessness and kindness throughout the entire book.

After journeying with her aging mother-in-law, Ruth enters Israel. This must have been very difficult for her as an outsider, from Moab no less. Indeed, we see that despite her allegiance to God and the Jewish people, many are reluctant to embrace her. This is reflected in the fact that throughout all four chapters of the book she is repeatedly referred to as a Moabite, despite her conversion. Yet Ruth only continues to impress us with her unusual spirit.

When they arrive in Bethlehem, Ruth realizes that the only way they would survive is if she would line up with the other paupers for charity handouts in the fields of the wealthy landowners. Judean society included many safety net programs to care for the poor and needy, as outlined in the Bible:

> *When you reap the harvest of your land, you shall not reap all the way to the edges of your field, or gather the gleanings of your harvest. You shall not pick your vineyard bare, or gather the fallen fruit of your vineyard; you shall leave them for the poor and the stranger: I the Hashem your God. (Leviticus 19:9-10)*

Nevertheless, it is never easy for the recipients of charity to swallow their pride and receive a handout. Perhaps the shame is too great for Naomi, which is why she doesn't accompany Ruth to the fields. Yet, Ruth volunteers to relinquish her dignity and gathers crops in the field to obtain food for herself and her mother-in-law.

Her selfless and unwavering commitment to Naomi continues when Ruth obediently follows her mother-in-law's unusual instructions:

> *"Now, Boaz, our relative, whose maidservants you have been with, is winnowing barley on the threshing floor tonight. Bathe and anoint yourself and put on your nicest clothing, and descend to the threshing floor. Yet, do not make yourself known to the man until he finishes eating and drinking. When he lies down, you will know the place where he lies. Come and uncover his feet and lie down. He will then tell you what you should do." (Ruth 3:2-4)*

Naomi tells Ruth to lie at the feet of Boaz in the middle of the night, putting her Moabite daughter-in-law in an uncomfortable position. Ruth has demonstrated that she distanced herself from Moabite behavior by being kind and dedicating herself to Naomi, and now Naomi was asking her to do something that could be perceived as sexually immoral - exactly the type of behavior that gave Moabite women their bad reputation. Yet Rut doesn't hesitate and obeys Naomi.

Finally, at the end of the story, after Ruth's dreams have come true and she finally finds security through marriage and a child, she immediately gives the child to Naomi to raise:

> *Naomi took the boy and she drew him towards her heart, and she took care of him. And the neighbors declared that it was as though a son had been born to Naomi. (Ruth 4:16-17)*

By giving up her maternal rights, the selfless heroine once again gives of herself for the sake of her mother-in-law. In each of the four chapters of the book, Ruth repeatedly sacrifices her own personal interests through her acts of generosity and kindness. From these repeated examples of kindness we see that Ruth overcomes her cruel national heritage and Moabite destiny, attaching herself instead to the people of Israel.

Yet despite her allegiance to Naomi and to God, and the many acts of kindness she displays throughout the story, many still see her as a Moabite. When a man who is a closer relative than Boaz, referred to as *Ploni Almoni* (the "anonymous" one), is given a chance to redeem Elimelech's property, he readily agrees. But when he discovers that he would also have to marry Ruth, he changes his mind (Ruth 4:6). This is, no doubt, a result of her Moabite origins, for, as we have mentioned earlier, Moabites were repugnant to the Jewish people and the Bible forbids them from marrying into the Jewish nation. However, the Sages teach that this prohibition applies only to Moabite men, and Moabite women who convert are, in fact, permitted to marry Jewish men. It is Boaz, someone who himself displays great kindness, who is able to see past her birthplace to the sterling character within. The union of these two personalities is the perfect formula from which the Davidic dynasty will arise.

To cast her lot with the Jewish people Ruth gave up everything familiar to her and was often treated as an outsider. But she recognized that there is something unique about the Jewish people, and she chose kindness and chosenness over comfort. As Rabbi Zeira says, she receives a great reward for her kindness, and ultimately finds that the benefits of her decision far outweigh any of the challenges and discomforts that she experiences along the way.

CHAPTER 3 - THE MOTHER OF REDEMPTION

The Book of Ruth is a story of redemption. By marrying Ruth, Boaz redeems her and her former husband by carrying on his family name, and also redeems the property that belonged to Elimelech and his family. However, the Book of Ruth is not only about the redemption of an individual, but of an entire nation, and even the entire world.

When Ruth confronts Boaz in the middle of the night on the threshing floor and asks him to redeem her through marriage, the concept of redemption is mentioned no less than 6 times:

> *However, although I am a* **redeemer***, there is another* **redeemer** *who is more closely related to you than I. Stay here tonight and, when it will be morning, if he will* **redeem** *you then fine, he may* **redeem** *you. Yet, if he does not desire to* **redeem** *you, I will* **redeem** *you. I swear, as Hashem lives. In the meanwhile, lie down until the morning. (Ruth 3:12-13)*

These verses refer not only to Ruth's personal redemption, but also allude to a redemption on a much broader scale. While Ruth appears to Boaz in the middle of the night, he tells her that the redemption will happen in the morning: "Stay for the night, then in the morning, if he will act as a redeemer, good!... Lie down until the morning."

The symbolic contrast of night and day are also found in the verses describing the Exodus from Egypt. There, the Bible writes that the liberation took place "in the middle of the night" (Exodus 12:29), yet later on in the same chapter it says that God took them out during the day: "at the end of the four hundred and thirtieth year, **in that very day**, all the ranks of Hashem departed from the land of Egypt" (Exodus 12:41). Similarly, in describing the future redemption of the Jewish people, Isaiah uses the theme of light and darkness to represent exile and redemption:

> *Arise, shine, for your light has dawned; The Presence of Hashem has shone upon you! Behold! Darkness shall cover the earth, And thick clouds the peoples; But upon you Hashem will shine, And His Presence be seen over you. And nations shall walk by your light, Kings, by your shining radiance. (Isaiah 60:1-3)*

By contrasting night and day, as the Bible does in these references to national redemption, the Book of Ruth is hinting that the redemption of Ruth will also lead to the redemption of the entire nation of Israel. This becomes clear at the end of the book, which describes the birth of Ruth and Boaz's child who, in turn, becomes the grandfather of King David, forefather of the Messiah.

Not only does God know that the personal redemption of Ruth will lead to the eventual redemption of the nation, the people of Bethlehem themselves express the hope that the union between Ruth and Boaz will lead to national redemption. After Boaz announces his intention to marry Ruth, the people present respond with the following blessing:

> *May Hashem enable the woman who is coming into your house to be like Rachel and like Leah, both of whom built the House of Yisrael. May you be successful in Efrat and may you perpetuate your name in Beit Lechem. (Ruth 4:11)*

They offer a blessing that Ruth should be like Rachel and Leah, who "both" built up the house of Israel.

Rachel and Leah each had their own challenges in their marriage to Jacob. Leah yearned for her husband's love and attention, while Rachel struggled to have children.

These challenges lead to a rivalry between the two sisters which is expressed in Leah's response to Rachel's request that she share the mandrakes found by her son Reuben: "Was it not enough for you to take away my husband, that you would also take my son's mandrakes?" (Genesis 30:15).

This rivalry and discord passed down to the next generation and divided their children. It led to the contention between Joseph and his brothers, which ended in the sale of Joseph to Egypt. And it found expression in the antagonism between Saul the Benjamite (son of Rachel), and David the Judean (son of Leah). The time of the judges, when the Book of Ruth takes place, was also a time of disunity. The expression, "In those days there was no king in Israel; everyone did as he pleased" (Judges 17:6, 21:25), is repeated more than once, implying that because there was no king to serve as a unifying force, there was a culture of "every man for himself." The book ends in the aftermath of a civil war, in which Benjamin is almost completely wiped out by the other tribes.

Nevertheless, Rachel and Leah are both credited, *together*, as being the mothers of the entire nation. The blessing bestowed upon Ruth and Boaz alludes to a calling for national harmony, which was sorely missing at that time. The people pray that this union will ultimately unite the nation.

David, the great-grandson of Ruth and Boaz, understood this need for unity. Despite descending from the line of Leah, he avoids using any violence towards King Saul, who sought to kill him. In his attempts at reconciliation with the family of Saul, he befriends Saul's son Jonathan and marries his daughter Michal. Later, when he became king, he moved his capital city from Hebron, in the center of the territory of Judah, to Jerusalem, which sat along the border of the territory of Benjamin.

David's attempts to unify the nation were initially successful, and when he became king he was recognized by "all the tribes of Israel" (II Samuel 5:1). However, two generations later, the nation was again divided when ten tribes pulled away from the Kingdom of Judah and formed their own Kingdom of Israel. But the hope for national unity has never been lost, and the prophets foretell of a time when the nation of Israel will again be reunited under the leadership of David's primary descendant, the Messiah.

Isaiah describes a future period when there will be no more rivalry, no more jealousy and no more envy between Judah and Ephraim (another name for the Kingdom of Israel):

> *But a shoot shall grow out of the stump of Jesse, A twig shall sprout from his stock. The spirit of Hashem shall alight upon him: a spirit of wisdom and insight, a spirit of counsel and valor, a spirit of devotion and reverence for Hashem. He shall sense the truth by his reverence for Hashem: He shall not judge by what his eyes behold, nor decide by what his ears perceive. Thus he shall judge the poor with equity and decide with justice for the lowly of the land. He shall strike down a land with the rod of his mouth and slay the wicked with the breath of his lips. Justice shall be the girdle of his loins, And faithfulness the girdle of his waist. The wolf shall dwell with the lamb, the leopard shall lie down with the kid; The calf, the beast of prey, and the fatling together, with a little boy to herd them. The cow and the bear*

shall graze, their young shall lie down together; and the lion, like the ox, shall eat straw. A babe shall play over a viper's hole, And an infant shall pass his hand over an adder's den. In all of My sacred mount nothing evil or vile shall be done; For the land shall be filled with devotion to Hashem, as water covers the sea. On that day, the stock of Jesse that has remained standing shall become a standard to peoples - nations shall seek his counsel and his abode shall be honored. On that day, Hashem will apply His hand again to redeeming the other part of His people from Assyria - as also from Egypt, Pathros, Nubia, Elam, Shinar, Hamath, and the coastlands. He will hold up a signal to the nations and assemble the banished of Israel, And gather the dispersed of Judah from the four corners of the earth. Then Ephraim's envy shall cease and Judah's harassment shall end; Ephraim shall not envy Judah, and Judah shall not harass Ephraim. (Isaiah 11:1-13)

When Ruth and Boaz's child is born, the women bless the baby with the hope that his name be perpetuated throughout *all* of Israel (Ruth 4:14). Naomi, not Ruth, raises the child. And it is the women who name the baby, not the mother. All this signals that the child, his name and his destiny, belong not to his immediate parents, but to the greater nation that he will serve.

The Book of Ruth ends with the genealogy of King David. Only a monarch who has inherited the kindness and compassion of Ruth and Boaz can bring about real national unity and the ultimate redemption.

CHAPTER 4 - FROM RUTH TO DAVID: THE FOUNDATIONS OF ROYALTY

Why was the Book of Ruth included in the canon of Hebrew Scriptures? As mentioned previously, according to the Talmudic sage Rabbi Zeira it is included "To teach us the greatness of the reward for acts of lovingkindness." However, there is another opinion that explains the need for this book. According to the *Zohar Chadash*, the Book of Ruth was written to present the lineage of King David. This is supported by the fact that the book concludes with the genealogy of King David:

> *Naomi took the boy and she drew him towards her heart, and she took care of him. And the neighbors declared that it was as though a son had been born to Naomi, and they called him Oved. He is the father of Yishai, who was the father of David. These are the generations of Peretz: Peretz fathered Chetzron. Chetzron fathered Ram, and Ram fathered Aminadav. Aminadav fathered Nachshon, and Nachshon fathered Salma. Salma fathered Boaz, and Boaz fathered Oved. Oved fathered Yishai, and Yishai fathered David. (Ruth 4:16-22)*

Other major characters in the Bible, such as Abraham, Moses and Samuel, are introduced with a genealogy. But more than just the origin story of a particular king, the genealogy here provides the origins of the very institution of Jewish monarchy. This is why the lineage is introduced with the phrase *v'eileh toldot*, "These are the generations of" (Ruth 4:18). While this phrase is commonly used in the Book of Genesis, it only appears twice in the rest of the Bible. The first is in Numbers 3, where it introduces the priestly genealogy, and the second is here, at the end of the Book of Ruth, where it introduces the royal genealogy. These two genealogies are the only two times that a family is selected for a specific role to lead the nation, and hence they are introduced with the same phrase.

There is a well known debate about the Bible's approach to monarchy. On the one hand, when the Jewish people request a king in the Book of Samuel, Samuel is very upset. God seems to agree with him that the request is inappropriate, and tells Samuel that in requesting a king they are rejecting God:

> *All the elders of Israel assembled and came to Samuel at Ramah, and they said to him, "You have grown old, and your sons have not followed your ways. Therefore appoint a king for us, to govern us like all other nations." Samuel was displeased that they said "Give us a king to govern us." Samuel prayed to Hashem, and Hashem replied to Samuel, "Heed the demand of the people in everything they say to you. For it is not you that they have rejected; it is Me they have rejected as their king. Like everything else they have done ever since I brought them out of Egypt to this day - forsaking Me and worshiping other gods - so they are doing to you. Heed their demand; but warn them solemnly, and tell them about the practices of any king who will rule over them." (I Samuel 8:-9)*

However, in Deuteronomy the Bible seems to allow, and some say even command, that the Jewish people appoint a king:

> *If, after you have entered the land that Hashem your God has assigned to you, and taken possession of it and settled in it, you decide, "I will set a king over me, as do all the nations about me," you shall be free to set a king over yourself, one chosen by Hashem your God. Be sure to set as king over yourself one of your own people; you must not set a foreigner over you, one who is not your kinsman. Moreover, he shall not keep many horses or send people back to Egypt to add to his horses, since Hashem has warned you, "You must not go back that way again." And he shall not have many wives, lest his heart go astray; nor shall he amass silver and gold to excess. When he is seated on his royal throne, he shall have a copy of this teaching written for him on a scroll by the levitical priests. Let it remain with him and let him read in it all his life, so that he may learn to revere Hashem his God, to observe faithfully every word of this teaching as well as these laws. Thus he will not act haughtily toward his fellows or deviate from the Instruction to the right or to the left, to the end that he and his descendants may reign long in the midst of Israel. (Deuteronomy 17:14-20)*

In fact, at the very beginning of the Bible we see that God considers monarchy a blessing. God promises Abraham that his descendants will be kings: "and kings shall come forth from you" (17:6). He makes a similar promise to Jacob: "kings shall issue from your loins" (Genesis 35:11).

Commentators explain that the legitimacy of a monarch hinges on the people's motivation in appointing the king. The problem in the Book of Samuel was that the people demanded a king in order "to govern us like all other nations." Since their motivation was to be like the other nations, the request was improper. However, if the purpose of appointing the king is to keep the people on the path of God, then such a king is not only legitimate but beneficial.

Throughout the Bible, however, we find uneasiness with monarchy. On the one hand, it is necessary to maintain order, an idea which is clearly expressed in the Book of Judges: "In those days there was no king in Israel; everyone did as he pleased" (Judges 17:6, 21:25). A king is also needed to further the national purpose of the Jewish people: to bring about a universal recognition of the Divine and to disseminate this recognition throughout the world. Succeeding in this mission requires a strong and stable government.

On the other hand, we see throughout the Bible that monarchy is fraught with challenges, and that concentrating the power of the kingdom into the hands of one individual has the potential to corrupt. Indeed, there was not even a single righteous king from among all of the northern Israelite kings! This is why the Bible places restrictions on the king, which are meant to serve as a system of checks and balances in order to keep the king on the right path and prevent him from abusing his power.

The Book of Ruth provides a solution and proper framework for the institution of monarchy. As we have shown previously, Ruth serves as an extreme example of kindness and selflessness. Through her actions, she models the type of behavior that is expected of a king of Israel. With this "kindness DNA" in their genetic makeup, the kings that descend from the Davidic line have a chance to overcome the challenges and temptations that come alongside absolute power. They have the ability to put aside their own egos in order to look out for the good of their subjects and their country, and to lead the people in their Divine mission of bringing Godliness and morality to the world.

With this understanding, we can reconcile the two reasons given for why the Book of Ruth was recorded in the Bible. It was written to teach the importance of kindness, as Rabbi Zeira asserts - and specifically the type of kindness that was essential to create and sustain the Davidic dynasty.

May we soon see the return of David's line, the redemption of Israel and the entire world!

Megillat Ruth: Questions for High School Students

POINTS TO PONDER:

1) The book begins with the words: And it was in the days when the judges judged (Ruth 1:1). Why is it significant that this story took place during the time of the Shoftim (Judges)? Sefer Shoftim (the Book of Judges) ends with the words "In those days there was no king in Israel; everyone did as he pleased." How might this be relevant to understanding the connection between the books of Judges and Ruth?

2) Elimelech moves his family from Israel to Moab in order to escape famine. In Moab, Elimelech dies, his two sons marry Moabite women and then his sons die as well. The verses seem to be telling us that Elimelech and his children were punished, and the sages say so explicitly. What was wrong with what Elimelech did? Why do you think he was punished? What about the rest of his family, what did they do wrong?

3) Rabbi Zeira teaches that the Book of Ruth was written in order to teach the great reward for doing chesed (loving-kindness).

4) How many examples of chesed can you find in the story? Who performs each of these acts of kindness and who is on the receiving end of each one? What is the great reward that they receive for doing chesed?

5) They say that doing kindness not only benefits the receiver but also the giver. How did everyone in the story benefit from kindness?

6) Naomi experiences the trauma of losing her entire immediate family and all of her wealth. Ruth becomes a foreigner in a foreign land who is shunned by most of her new neighbors (she is constantly called a Moabite, and the closest relative who is eligible to redeem her does not want to marry her lest he "ruin" his estate (Ruth 4:6)). How did chesed help them each overcome their individual traumas? How can we use chesed to help people that we know who are going through a difficult situation?

7) The rabbis teach us that doing a mitzvah, performing one of God's commandments, leads to the performance of more commandments. This can be seen with the performance of kindness in the Book of Ruth. How does performing acts of kindness lead to more kindness in the Book of Ruth? Can you think of examples of this from your own lives?

8) The book ends with the birth of King David. In what way might the birth of King David be an appropriate ending for the book? Why was the birth of David the appropriate reward for Ruth and Boaz? How might the institution of monarchy be a solution, or resolution, to some of the issues that arise in the book of Ruth?

9) What lessons about leadership and responsibility can we learn from the Book of Ruth? How can we apply these ideas to our own lives?

1  א

And it was in the days when the judges judged that there was a famine in the land. A man from *Beit Lechem*, in the territory of *Yehuda*, went to live in the fields of Moab – he, his wife, and their two sons.	*Vayehi bimei sh'fot ha'shoftim vayehi ra'av ba'aretz vayeilech ish mi'Beit Lechem Yehudah lagur bisdei mo'av hu ve'ishto ush'nei banav*	וַיְהִי, בִּימֵי שְׁפֹט הַשֹּׁפְטִים, וַיְהִי רָעָב, בָּאָרֶץ; וַיֵּלֶךְ אִישׁ מִבֵּית לֶחֶם יְהוּדָה, לָגוּר בִּשְׂדֵי מוֹאָב-- הוּא וְאִשְׁתּוֹ, וּשְׁנֵי בָנָיו.
The name of the man was *Elimelech*, the name of his wife was *Naomi*, and the names of his two sons were *Machlon* and *Kilyon*. They were from *Efrat* in the region of *Beit Lechem*, which was in the territory of *Yehuda*. They came to the field of Moab and were there.	*Vesheim ha'ish Elimelech vesheim ishto Na'omi vesheim sh'nei banav Machlon ve'Chilyon Efra'tim mi'Beit Lechem Yehudah vayavo'u s'dei-Mo'av vayehiyu-sham*	וְשֵׁם הָאִישׁ אֱלִימֶלֶךְ וְשֵׁם אִשְׁתּוֹ נָעֳמִי וְשֵׁם שְׁנֵי-בָנָיו מַחְלוֹן וְכִלְיוֹן, אֶפְרָתִים-- מִבֵּית לֶחֶם, יְהוּדָה; וַיָּבֹאוּ שְׂדֵי-מוֹאָב, וַיִּהְיוּ-שָׁם.
Elimelech, the husband of *Naomi*, died, and she and her two sons remained.	*Vayamot Elimelech ish Naomi vatisha'eir hi ush'nei vaneha*	וַיָּמָת אֱלִימֶלֶךְ, אִישׁ נָעֳמִי; וַתִּשָּׁאֵר הִיא, וּשְׁנֵי בָנֶיהָ.

4 | They married women from Moab. The name of one was *Orpah* and the name of the second was *Rut,* and they settled there for about ten years. | *Vayis'u lahem nashim Mo'aviyot sheim ha'achat Orpah vesheim hasheinit Rut vayeish'vu sham k'esar shanim* | וַיִּשְׂאוּ לָהֶם, נָשִׁים מֹאֲבִיּוֹת--שֵׁם הָאַחַת עָרְפָּה, וְשֵׁם הַשֵּׁנִית רוּת; וַיֵּשְׁבוּ שָׁם, כְּעֶשֶׂר שָׁנִים. | ד

5 | *Machlon* and *Kilyon* died as well, and the woman was bereft of her two children and her husband. | *Vayamutu gam sh'neihem Machlon v'Chilyon vatisha'er ha'ishah mish'nei y'ladeha umei'ishah* | וַיָּמֻתוּ גַם-שְׁנֵיהֶם, מַחְלוֹן וְכִלְיוֹן; וַתִּשָּׁאֵר, הָאִשָּׁה, מִשְּׁנֵי יְלָדֶיהָ, וּמֵאִישָׁהּ. | ה

6 | She and her daughters-in-law then rose to return from the fields of Moab, since she heard in the fields of Moab that *Hashem* had recalled His nation to give them bread. | *Vatakam hi v'cheloteha vateshav mis'dei Mo'av ki sham'ah bisdei mo'av ki-fakad a-do-nai et-amo lateit lahem lachem* | וַתָּקָם הִיא וְכַלֹּתֶיהָ, וַתָּשָׁב מִשְּׂדֵי מוֹאָב: כִּי שָׁמְעָה, בִּשְׂדֵה מוֹאָב-- כִּי-פָקַד יְהוָה אֶת-עַמּוֹ, לָתֵת לָהֶם לָחֶם. | ו

7 | She went out from the place where she had been with her two daughters-in-law, and they walked on the road to the land of *Yehuda.* | *Vateitzei min-hamakom asher hay'ta-shama ush'tei kaloteha imah vateilachnah vaderech lashuv el-eretz Yehudah* | וַתֵּצֵא, מִן-הַמָּקוֹם אֲשֶׁר הָיְתָה-שָׁמָּה, וּשְׁתֵּי כַלּוֹתֶיהָ, עִמָּהּ; וַתֵּלַכְנָה בַדֶּרֶךְ, לָשׁוּב אֶל-אֶרֶץ יְהוּדָה. | ז

8 | *Naomi* then said to her two daughters-in-law, "let each of you go and return to her mother's house. May *Hashem* do acts of kindness for you just as you have done for the deceased and for me. | *Vatomer Naomi lishtei chaloteha leichnah shovnah ishah leveit imah ya'as Adonai imachem chesed ka'asher asitem im-hameitim v'imadi* | וַתֹּאמֶר נָעֳמִי, לִשְׁתֵּי כַלֹּתֶיהָ, לֵכְנָה שֹּׁבְנָה, אִשָּׁה לְבֵית אִמָּהּ; יעשה (יַעַשׂ) יְהוָה עִמָּכֶם חֶסֶד, כַּאֲשֶׁר עֲשִׂיתֶם עִם-הַמֵּתִים וְעִמָּדִי. | ח

9   May *Hashem* grant that you should find respite, each of you in the home of her new husband." She then kissed them and they lifted their voices and cried.

Yitein Adonai lachem umtzena menuchah ishah beit ishah vatishak lah'en vatisenah kolan vativkenah

יִתֵּן יְהוָה, לָכֶם,
וּמְצֶאןָ מְנוּחָה, אִשָּׁה
בֵּית אִישָׁהּ; וַתִּשַּׁק
לָהֶן, וַתִּשֶּׂאנָה קוֹלָן
וַתִּבְכֶּינָה.   ט

10   They said to her, "No, we will return with you to your people."

Vatomarnah lah ki itach nashuv l'ameich

וַתֹּאמַרְנָה-לָּהּ: כִּי-אִתָּךְ
נָשׁוּב, לְעַמֵּךְ.   י

11   However, *Naomi* said, "Return, my daughters. Why would you come with me? Do I have more sons within me who could become your husbands?

Vatomer Naomi shovnah v'notai lamah teilachnah imi ha'od-li vanim b'mei'ai v'hayu lachem la'anashim

וַתֹּאמֶר נָעֳמִי שֹׁבְנָה
בְנֹתַי, לָמָּה תֵלַכְנָה
עִמִּי: הַעוֹד-לִי בָנִים
בְּמֵעַי, וְהָיוּ לָכֶם
לַאֲנָשִׁים.   יא

12   Return, my daughters. Go, for I am too old to have a husband. Even if I would say that there is hope for me, and even if I were to have a husband this night and even if I would have more sons,

Shovnah v'notai leichna ki zakanti mih'yot l'ish ki amarti yesh-li tikvah gam hayiti halailah l'ish v'gam yaladti vanim

שֹׁבְנָה בְנֹתַי לֵכְןָ, כִּי
זָקַנְתִּי מִהְיוֹת לְאִישׁ:
כִּי אָמַרְתִּי, יֶשׁ-לִי
תִקְוָה--גַּם הָיִיתִי
הַלַּיְלָה לְאִישׁ, וְגַם
יָלַדְתִּי בָנִים.   יב

13 would you wait for them until they matured? Would you bind yourselves to them and not marry anyone else? No, my daughters. For it is much more bitter for me than for you, for the hand of *Hashem* has gone out against me."

Halahein t'shabeirnah ad asher yigdalu halahein tei'ageinah l'vilti heyot l'ish al b'notai ki-mar-li m'od mikem ki-yatz'ah vi yad Adonai

הֲלָהֵן תְּשַׂבֵּרְנָה, עַד אֲשֶׁר יִגְדָּלוּ, הֲלָהֵן תֵּעָגֵנָה, לְבִלְתִּי הֱיוֹת לְאִישׁ; אַל בְּנֹתַי, כִּי-מַר-לִי מְאֹד מִכֶּם--כִּי-יָצְאָה בִי, יַד-יְהוָה. יג

14 They lifted their voices and cried extensively. *Orpah* kissed her mother-in-law, yet *Rut* stuck with her.

Vatisenah kolan vativkenah od vatishak Orpah lachamotah v'Rut davkah bah

וַתִּשֶּׂנָה קוֹלָן, וַתִּבְכֶּינָה עוֹד; וַתִּשַּׁק עָרְפָּה לַחֲמוֹתָהּ, וְרוּת דָּבְקָה בָּהּ. יד

15 In response, she said, "Look, your sister-in-law has returned to her people and her gods. Follow after your sister-in-law."

Vatomer hinei shavah y'vimteich el amah v'el elohehah shuvi acharei y'vimteich

וַתֹּאמֶר, הִנֵּה שָׁבָה יְבִמְתֵּךְ, אֶל-עַמָּהּ, וְאֶל-אֱלֹהֶיהָ; שׁוּבִי, אַחֲרֵי יְבִמְתֵּךְ. טו

16 However, *Rut* said, "Do not compel me to leave you, to turn back from following after you. For where you go, I will go, and where you stay, I will stay. Your nation is my nation and your God is my God.

Vatomer Rut al-tifg'i-vi l'azveich lashuv mei'acharayich ki el-asher teil'chi eileich uva'asher talini alin ameich ami vEilohayich Elohai

וַתֹּאמֶר רוּת אַל-תִּפְגְּעִי-בִי, לְעָזְבֵךְ לָשׁוּב מֵאַחֲרָיִךְ: כִּי אֶל-אֲשֶׁר תֵּלְכִי אֵלֵךְ, וּבַאֲשֶׁר תָּלִינִי אָלִין--עַמֵּךְ עַמִּי, וֵאלֹהַיִךְ אֱלֹהָי. טז

17 Where you will die, I will die and I will be buried there. May *Hashem* do so for me, and even more, for only death will separate between me and you."

Ba'asher tamuti amut v'sham ekaveir koh ya'aseh Adonai li v'choh yosif ki hamavet yafrid beini uveineich

בַּאֲשֶׁר תָּמוּתִי אָמוּת, וְשָׁם אֶקָּבֵר; כֹּה יַעֲשֶׂה יְהוָה לִי, וְכֹה יוֹסִיף-- כִּי הַמָּוֶת, יַפְרִיד בֵּינִי וּבֵינֵךְ. יז

18 When she saw that *Rut* was determined to travel with her, she stopped trying to dissuade her.

Vateire ki-mitametzet hi lalechet itah vatechdal l'daber eileha

וַתֵּרֶא, כִּי-מִתְאַמֶּצֶת הִיא לָלֶכֶת אִתָּהּ; וַתֶּחְדַּל, לְדַבֵּר אֵלֶיהָ. יח

19 The two of them traveled until they came to *Beit Lechem*. And it was when they entered *Beit Lechem* that the entire city was astonished over them and proclaimed, "Is this *Naomi*?"

Vateilachnah sh'teihem ad-bo'anah Beit Lechem vaihi k'vo'anah beit lechem vateihom kol-ha'ir aleihen vatomarnah hazot Naomi

וַתֵּלַכְנָה שְׁתֵּיהֶם, עַד-בּוֹאָנָה בֵּית לָחֶם; וַיְהִי, כְּבוֹאָנָה בֵּית לֶחֶם, וַתֵּהֹם כָּל-הָעִיר עֲלֵיהֶן, וַתֹּאמַרְנָה הֲזֹאת נָעֳמִי. יט

20 She said to them, "Do not call me *Naomi*, but rather call me "*Mara*," for *Shaddai* has made me exceedingly bitter."

Vatomer aleihen al-tikrenah li Naomi k'rena li Mara ki-heimar Shaddai li m'od

וַתֹּאמֶר אֲלֵיהֶן, אַל-תִּקְרֶאנָה לִי נָעֳמִי: קְרֶאןָ לִי מָרָא, כִּי-הֵמַר שַׁדַּי לִי מְאֹד. כ

21 I was full when I moved, but *Hashem* has returned me empty. Why should you refer to me as *Naomi* when *Hashem* has rejoined me; *Shaddai* has generated calamity for me."

Ani m'lei'ah halachti v'reikam heshivani Adonai lamah tikrenah li Na'omi vadonai anah vi v'Shaddai heira li

אֲנִי מְלֵאָה הָלַכְתִּי, וְרֵיקָם הֱשִׁיבַנִי יְהוָה; לָמָּה תִקְרֶאנָה לִי, נָעֳמִי, וַיהוָה עָנָה בִי, וְשַׁדַּי הֵרַע לִי. כא

22 So *Naomi* returned, and *Rut,* her Moabite daughter-in-law, with her, from the fields of Moab, and they came to *Beit Lechem* at the start of the barley harvest.

Vatashov na'omi v'Rut haMo'aviyah chalatah imah hashavah mis'dei Moav v'heimah ba'u Beit Lechem bitchilat k'tzir s'orim

וַתָּשׇׁב נָעֳמִי, וְרוּת הַמּוֹאֲבִיָּה כַלָּתָהּ עִמָּהּ, הַשָּׁבָה, מִשְּׂדֵי מוֹאָב; וְהֵמָּה, בָּאוּ בֵּית לֶחֶם, בִּתְחִלַּת, קְצִיר שְׂעֹרִים. כב

2

ב

1 Now *Naomi* had a family member through her husband, who was a powerful and courageous man from the family of *Elimelech,* and his name was *Boaz.*

UlNaomi moda l'ishah ish gibor chayil mimishpachat Elimlech ush'mo Boaz

וּלְנָעֳמִי מידע (מוֹדָע) לְאִישָׁהּ, אִישׁ גִּבּוֹר חַיִל--מִמִּשְׁפַּחַת, אֱלִימֶלֶךְ; וּשְׁמוֹ, בֹּעַז. א

2 *Rut* the Moabite said to *Naomi,* "I will go, with your consent, to the field, and collect from among the ears of grain after one in whose eyes I will find favor." And *Naomi* replied, "Go, my daughter."

Vatomer Rut haMoaviyah el-Naomi eil'cha-na hasadeh va'alakatah vashibalim achar asher emtza-chein b'einav vatomer lah l'chi viti

וַתֹּאמֶר רוּת הַמּוֹאֲבִיָּה אֶל-נָעֳמִי, אֵלְכָה-נָּא הַשָּׂדֶה וַאֲלַקֳטָה בַשִּׁבֳּלִים--אַחַר, אֲשֶׁר אֶמְצָא-חֵן בְּעֵינָיו; וַתֹּאמֶר לָהּ, לְכִי בִתִּי. ב

3 | She went and came and collected after the harvesters in the field. It happened that she chanced upon the section of land that belonged to *Boaz*, who was from the family of *Elimelech*. | *Vateilech vatavo vat'laket basadeh acharei hakotz'rim vayiker mikreh chelkat hasadeh l'Voaz asher mimishpachat Elimlech* | וַתֵּלֶךְ וַתָּבוֹא וַתְּלַקֵּט בַּשָּׂדֶה, אַחֲרֵי הַקֹּצְרִים; וַיִּקֶר מִקְרֶהָ--חֶלְקַת הַשָּׂדֶה לְבֹעַז, אֲשֶׁר מִמִּשְׁפַּחַת אֱלִימֶלֶךְ. | ג

4 | Behold, *Boaz* came from *Beit Lechem* and he greeted the harvesters and said, "May *Hashem* be with you!" And they replied, "May *Hashem* bless you!" | *V'hinei-Voaz ba miBeit Lechem vayomer lakotz'rim Adonai imachem vayom'ru lo y'varech'cha Adonai* | וְהִנֵּה-בֹעַז, בָּא מִבֵּית לֶחֶם, וַיֹּאמֶר לַקּוֹצְרִים, יְהוָה עִמָּכֶם; וַיֹּאמְרוּ לוֹ, יְבָרֶכְךָ יְהוָה. | ד

5 | *Boaz* then asked his servant, who stood in charge over the harvesters, "To whom does this young woman belong?" | *Vayomer Boaz l'na'aro hanitzav al-hakotz'rim l'mi hana'arah hazot* | וַיֹּאמֶר בֹּעַז לְנַעֲרוֹ, הַנִּצָּב עַל-הַקּוֹצְרִים: לְמִי, הַנַּעֲרָה הַזֹּאת. | ה

6 | The servant who stood in charge of the harvesters answered and affirmed, "She is a Moabite who has returned with *Naomi* from the field of Moab. | *Vaya'an hana'ar hanitzav al-hakotz'rim vayomer na'arah mo'aviyah hi hashavah im-Na'omi mis'dei Moav* | וַיַּעַן, הַנַּעַר הַנִּצָּב עַל-הַקּוֹצְרִים--וַיֹּאמַר: נַעֲרָה מוֹאֲבִיָּה הִיא, הַשָּׁבָה עִם-נָעֳמִי מִשְּׂדֵי מוֹאָב. | ו

7

She said, 'I will go, with your consent, to collect and gather the ears of grain left after the harvesters.' She came and has been standing from the morning until now, with the exception of resting in the house for a little bit."

Vatomer alakatah-na v'asafti va'amarim acharei hakotz'rim vatavo vata'amod mei'az haboker v'ad-atah zeh shivtah habayit m'at

וַתֹּאמֶר, אֲלַקֳטָה-נָּא וְאָסַפְתִּי בָעֳמָרִים, אַ חֲרֵי, הַקּוֹצְרִים; וַתָּב וֹא וַתַּעֲמוֹד, מֵאָז הַבֹּקֶר וְעַד-עַתָּה--זֶה שִׁבְתָּהּ הַבַּיִת, מְעָט.

ז

8

Boaz then said to *Rut*, "Listen to me, my daughter. Do not collect in another field and please do not move from here. Rather, remain in close proximity to my maidservants.

Vayomer Boaz el-Rut halo shama'at biti al-teil'chi lilkot basadeh acheir v'gam lo ta'avuri mizeh v'cho tidbakim im-na'arotai

וַיֹּאמֶר בֹּעַז אֶל-רוּת הֲלוֹא שָׁמַעַתְּ בִּתִּי, אַ ל-תֵּלְכִי לִלְקֹט בְּשָׂדֶה אַחֵר, וְגַם לֹא תַעֲבוּ רִי, מִזֶּה; וְכֹה תִדְבָּקִין, עִם-נַעֲרֹתָי.

ח

9

Place your eyes on the field in which they will harvest, and follow them. I have ordered young men not to touch you. When you are thirsty, walk to the containers and drink from the water that the young men have drawn."

Einayich basadeh asher-yiktzorun v'halachti achareihen halo tziviti et-han'arim l'vilti nog'eich v'tzamit v'halacht' el-hakeilim v'shatit mei'asher yishavun han'arim

עֵינַיִךְ בַּשָּׂדֶה אֲשֶׁר-י קְצֹרוּן, וְהָלַכְתִּ אַ חֲרֵיהֶן--הֲלוֹא צִוִּיתִי אֶת-הַנְּעָרִים, לְבִלְתִּי נָגְעֵךְ; וְצָמִת, וְהָלַכְתְּ אֶל-הַכֵּלִים, וְשָׁתִית, מֵאֲשֶׁר יִשְׁאֲבוּן הַנְּעָרִים.

ט

10 *Rut* fell upon her face, and bowed to the ground. She then said to him, "Why have I found favor in your eyes so that you distinguish me with preferential treatment when I am a stranger?"

Vatipol al-paneha vatishtachu ar'tza vatomer eilav madua matzati chein b'einecha l'hakireini v'anochi nochriyah

וַתִּפֹּל, עַל-פָּנֶיהָ, וַתִּשְׁתַּחוּ, אָרְצָה; וַתֹּאמֶר אֵלָיו, מַדּוּעַ מָצָאתִי חֵן בְּעֵינֶיךָ לְהַכִּירֵנִי--וְאָנֹכִי, נָכְרִיָּה. י

11 *Boaz* answered and said to her, "All that you have done for your mother-in-law following the death of your husband has been related to me; how you left your father and mother and the land of your birth, and joined a nation that you did not know yesterday or beforehand.

Vaya'an Boaz vayomer lah higad hugad li kol asher-asit et-chamoteich acharei mot isheich vata'azvi avich v'imeich v'eretz moladteich vateil'chi el-am asher lo-yada'at t'mol shilshom

וַיַּעַן בֹּעַז, וַיֹּאמֶר לָהּ--הֻגֵּד הֻגַּד לִי כֹּל אֲשֶׁר-עָשִׂית אֶת-חֲמוֹתֵךְ, אַחֲרֵי מוֹת אִישֵׁךְ; וַתַּעַזְבִי אָבִיךְ וְאִמֵּךְ, וְאֶרֶץ מוֹלַדְתֵּךְ, וַתֵּלְכִי, אֶל-עַם אֲשֶׁר לֹא-יָדַעַתְּ תְּמוֹל שִׁלְשׁוֹם. יא

12 May *Hashem* repay you for your actions and may you be fully rewarded from *Hashem*, the God of *Yisrael*, under Whose wings you have come for protection."

Y'shaleim Adonai pa'aleich ut'hi maskurteich sh'leima mei'im Adonai Elohei Yisrael asher-bat lachasot tachat-k'nafav

יְשַׁלֵּם יְהוָה, פָּעֳלֵךְ; וּתְהִי מַשְׂכֻּרְתֵּךְ שְׁלֵמָה, מֵעִם יְהוָה אֱלֹהֵי יִשְׂרָאֵל, אֲשֶׁר-בָּאת, לַחֲסוֹת תַּחַת-כְּנָפָיו. יב

13 She replied with gratitude, "I have found favor in your eyes, my master, for you have consoled me and spoken to the heart of your maidservant and, yet, I am not even like one of your maidservants.

Vatomer emtza-chein b'einecha adoni ki nichamtani v'chi dibarta al-leiv shifchatecha v'anochi lo ehyeh k'achat shifchotecha

וַתֹּאמֶר אֶמְצָא-חֵן בְּעֵינֶיךָ אֲדֹנִי, כִּי נִחַמְתָּנִי, וְכִי דִבַּרְתָּ, עַל-לֵב שִׁפְחָתֶךָ; וְאָנֹכִי לֹא אֶהְיֶה, כְּאַחַת שִׁפְחֹתֶיךָ. יג

14 When it was time to eat, *Boaz* said to her, "Come forward and eat from the communal bread. Dip your piece in vinegar." So she sat next to the harvesters and he gave her some roasted grain, of which she ate until she was satisfied and even had some left over.

Vayomer lah Voaz l'eit ha'ochel goshi halom v'achalt min-halechem v'tavalt piteich bachometz vateishev mitzad hakotz'rim vayitzbat-lah kali vatochal vatisba vatotar

וַיֹּאמֶר לָה בֹעַז לְעֵת הָאֹכֶל, גֹּשִׁי הֲלֹם וְאָכַלְתְּ מִן-הַלֶּחֶם, וְטָבַלְתְּ פִּתֵּךְ, בַּחֹמֶץ; וַתֵּשֶׁב, מִצַּד הַקֹּצְרִים, וַיִּצְבָּט-לָה קָלִי, וַתֹּאכַל וַתִּשְׂבַּע וַתֹּתַר. יד

15 When *Rut* rose to gather the discarded crops, *Boaz* directed his servants saying, "Have her collect even from the bundles and do not disgrace her.

Vatakam lilakeit vay'tzav boaz et-n'arav leimor gam bein ha'omarim t'laket v'lo tachlimuha

וַתָּקָם, לְלַקֵּט; וַיְצַו בֹּעַז אֶת-נְעָרָיו לֵאמֹר, גַּם בֵּין הָעֳמָרִים תְּלַקֵּט--וְלֹא תַכְלִימוּהָ. טו

16
Furthermore, take out some bundles from the piles for her and leave them so that she can collect them. Do not object to her."

V'gam shol-tasholu lah min-hatz'vatim va'azavtem v'lik'ta v'lo tigaru-vah

וְגַם שֹׁל-תָּשֹׁלּוּ לָהּ, מִן-הַצְּבָתִים; וַעֲזַבְתֶּם וְלִקְּטָה, וְלֹא תִגְעֲרוּ-בָהּ. טז

17
She collected in the field until evening, and she beat that which she collected, which yielded approximately one ephah of barley.

Vat'lakeit basadeh ad-ha'arev vatachbot eit asher-likeitah vaihi k'eifah s'orim

וַתְּלַקֵּט בַּשָּׂדֶה, עַד-הָעָרֶב; וַתַּחְבֹּט אֵת אֲשֶׁר-לִקֵּטָה, וַיְהִי כְּאֵיפָה שְׂעֹרִים. יז

18
Rut carried it and arrived at the city. Her mother-in-law saw what she had collected, and *Rut* took some grain out to give her from that which remained after she had eaten her fill.

Vatisa vatavo ha'ir vateira chamotah eit asher-likeitah vatotzei vatiten-lah eit asher-hotirah misav'ah

וַתִּשָּׂא וַתָּבוֹא הָעִיר, וַתֵּרֶא חֲמוֹתָהּ אֵת אֲשֶׁר-לִקֵּטָה; וַתּוֹצֵא, וַתִּתֶּן-לָהּ, אֵת אֲשֶׁר-הוֹתִרָה, מִשָּׂבְעָהּ. יח

19
Her mother-in-law inquired, "Where did you collect today and where did you accomplish this? May the one who recognized you with such kindness be blessed!" *Rut* told her mother-in-law in whose field she had done this work and said, "The name of the man that I worked with is *Boaz*."

Vatomer lah chamotah eifoh likat't hayom v'anah asit yehi makireich baruch vatageid lachamotah eit asher-as'ta imo vatomer sheim ha'ish asher asiti imo hayom Boaz

וַתֹּאמֶר לָהּ חֲמוֹתָהּ אֵיפֹה לִקַּטְתְּ הַיּוֹם, וְאָנָה עָשִׂית--יְהִי מַכִּירֵךְ, בָּרוּךְ; וַתַּגֵּד לַחֲמוֹתָהּ, אֵת אֲשֶׁר-עָשְׂתָה עִמּוֹ, וַתֹּאמֶר שֵׁם הָאִישׁ אֲשֶׁר עָשִׂיתִי עִמּוֹ הַיּוֹם, בֹּעַז. יט

20

Naomi then said to her daughter-in-law, "Blessed is he before *Hashem*, for he has not forsaken his kindness to the living or the dead. Furthermore, *Naomi* said to her, "He is our relative who is eligible to redeem us."

Vatomer Naomi l'chalatah baruch hu l'Adonai asher lo-azav chasdo et-hachayim v'et-hameitim vatomer lah Na'omi karov lanu ha'ish migoaleinu hu

וַתֹּאמֶר נָעֳמִי לְכַלָּתָהּ, בָּרוּךְ הוּא לַיהֹוָה, אֲשֶׁר לֹא-עָזַב חַסְדּוֹ, אֶת-הַחַיִּים וְאֶת-הַמֵּתִים; וַתֹּאמֶר לָהּ נָעֳמִי, קָרוֹב לָנוּ הָאִישׁ--מִגֹּאֲלֵנוּ, הוּא. כ

21

Rut the Moabite said, "Furthermore, he said to me, 'remain close to my workers until they have finished harvesting that which is mine.'"

Vatomer Rut haMoaviyah gam ki-amar eilai im-han'arim asher-li tidbakin ad im-kilu eit kol-hakatzir asher-li

וַתֹּאמֶר, רוּת הַמּוֹאֲבִיָּה: גַּם כִּי-אָמַר אֵלַי, עִם-הַנְּעָרִים אֲשֶׁר-לִי תִּדְבָּקִין, עַד אִם-כִּלּוּ, אֵת כָּל-הַקָּצִיר אֲשֶׁר-לִי. כא

22

Naomi then said to her daughter-in-law *Rut*, "It is good, my daughter, that you will go out with his maidservants rather than being harassed by others in a different field."

Vatomer Noami el-Rut kalatah tov biti ki teitz'i im-na'arotav v'lo yifg'u-vach b'sadeh acheir

וַתֹּאמֶר נָעֳמִי, אֶל-רוּת כַּלָּתָהּ: טוֹב בִּתִּי, כִּי תֵצְאִי עִם-נַעֲרוֹתָיו, וְלֹא יִפְגְּעוּ-בָךְ, בְּשָׂדֶה אַחֵר. כב

23

So she remained close to the maidservants of *Boaz* in order to collect grain until the barley and wheat harvests were over, and she continued to live with her mother-in-law.

Vatidbak b'na'arot Boaz lilakeit ad-k'lot k'tzir-has'orim vktzir hachitim vateishev et-chamotah

וַתִּדְבַּק בְּנַעֲרוֹת בֹּעַז, לְלַקֵּט--עַד-כְּלוֹת קְצִיר-הַשְּׂעֹרִים, וּקְצִיר הַחִטִּים; וַתֵּשֶׁב, אֶת-חֲמוֹתָהּ. כג

3

1	*Naomi*, her mother-in-law, said to her, "My daughter, I will seek to help you settle, which will be good for you.	*Vatomer lah Noami chamotah biti halo avakeish-lach manoach asher yiytav-lach*	וַתֹּאמֶר לָהּ, נָעֳמִי חֲמוֹתָהּ: בִּתִּי, הֲלֹא אֲבַקֶּשׁ-לָךְ מָנוֹחַ אֲשֶׁר יִיטַב-לָךְ.

א

2	Now, *Boaz*, our relative, whose maidservants you have been with, is winnowing barley on the threshing floor tonight.	*V'atah halo Voaz modatanu asher hayit et-na'arotav hineih-hu zoreh et-goren has'orim halailah*	וְעַתָּה, הֲלֹא בֹעַז מֹדַעְתָּנוּ, אֲשֶׁר הָיִית, אֶת-נַעֲרוֹתָיו; הִנֵּה-הוּא, זֹרֶה אֶת-גֹּרֶן הַשְּׂעֹרִים--הַלָּיְלָה.

ב

3	Bathe and anoint yourself and put on your nicest clothing, and descend to the threshing floor. Yet, do not make yourself known to the man until he finishes eating and drinking.	*V'rachatzt v'sacht v'samt simlotayich alayich v'yaradt hagoren al-tivad'i la'ish ad kaloto le'echol v'lishtot*	וְרָחַצְתְּ וָסַכְתְּ, וְשַׂמְתְּ שמלתך (שִׂמְלֹתַיִךְ) עָלַיִךְ--וירדתי (וְיָרַדְתְּ) הַגֹּרֶן; אַל-תִּוָּדְעִי לָאִישׁ, עַד כַּלֹּתוֹ לֶאֱכֹל וְלִשְׁתּוֹת.

ג

4	When he lies down, you will know the place where he lies. Come and uncover his feet and lie down. He will then tell you what you should do."	*Vihi b'shach'vo v'yada'at et-hamakom asher yishkav-sham uvat v'gilit marg'lotav vishachavt v'hu yagid lach eit asher ta'asin*	וִיהִי בְשָׁכְבוֹ, וְיָדַעַתְּ אֶת-הַמָּקוֹם אֲשֶׁר יִשְׁכַּב-שָׁם, וּבָאת וְגִלִּית מַרְגְּלֹתָיו, ושכבתי (וְשָׁכָבְתְּ); וְהוּא יַגִּיד לָךְ, אֵת אֲשֶׁר תַּעֲשִׂין.

ד

5	*Rut* replied, "I will do all that you say to me."	*Vatomer eileha kol asher-tom'ri aylai e'eseh*	וַתֹּאמֶר, אֵלֶיהָ: כֹּל אֲשֶׁר־תֹּאמְרִי (אֵלַי), אֶעֱשֶׂה.	ה
6	So she went down to the threshing floor and did all that her mother-in-law directed her.	*Vateired hagoren vata'as k'chol asher-tzivatah chamotah*	וַתֵּרֶד, הַגֹּרֶן; וַתַּעַשׂ, כְּכֹל אֲשֶׁר־צִוַּתָּה חֲמוֹתָהּ.	ו
7	*Boaz* ate and drank, and was in a cheerful spirit, and he came to lie down at the edge of piles of grain. She came quietly, uncovered his feet and lay down.	*Vayochal Boaz vayeisht vayitav libo vayavo lishkav biktzeih ha'areimah vatavo valat vat'gal marg'lotav vatishkav*	וַיֹּאכַל בֹּעַז וַיֵּשְׁתְּ, וַיִּיטַב לִבּוֹ, וַיָּבֹא, לִשְׁכַּב בִּקְצֵה הָעֲרֵמָה; וַתָּבֹא בַלָּט, וַתְּגַל מַרְגְּלֹתָיו וַתִּשְׁכָּב.	ז
8	In the middle of the night the man was alarmed, and he turned over. He was surprised to see that a woman was lying at his feet.	*Vaihi bachatzi halailah vayecherad ha'ish vayilafeit v'hineih ishah shochevet marg'lotav*	וַיְהִי בַּחֲצִי הַלַּיְלָה, וַיֶּחֱרַד הָאִישׁ וַיִּלָּפֵת; וְהִנֵּה אִשָּׁה, שֹׁכֶבֶת מַרְגְּלֹתָיו.	ח
9	He said, "Who are you?" She replied, "I am *Rut*, your maidservant." Spread your robe over your maidservant, for you are a redeemer."	*Vayomer mi-at vatomer anochi Rut amatecha ufarasta ch'nafecha al-amat'cha ki go'eil atah*	וַיֹּאמֶר, מִי־אָתְּ; וַתֹּאמֶר, אָנֹכִי רוּת אֲמָתֶךָ, וּפָרַשְׂתָּ כְנָפֶךָ עַל־אֲמָתְךָ, כִּי גֹאֵל אָתָּה.	ט

10 | He replied, "Blessed are you to *Hashem*, my daughter! Your most recent act of kindness is better than your first, in that you did not go after the young men whether poor or wealthy. | *Vayomer b'ruchah at l'Adonai biti heitavt chasdeich ha'acharon min-harishon l'vilti-lechet acharei habachurim im-dal v'im-ashir* | וַיֹּאמֶר, בְּרוּכָה אַתְּ לַיהוָה בִּתִּי--הֵיטַבְתְּ חַסְדֵּךְ הָאַחֲרוֹן, מִן-הָרִאשׁוֹן: לְבִלְתִּי-לֶכֶת, אַחֲרֵי הַבַּחוּרִים--אִם-דַּל, וְאִם-עָשִׁיר. | י

11 | Now, my daughter, do not be afraid. Everything that you have said I will do for you, for everyone in the gate of my people knows that you are a praiseworthy woman. | *V'atah biti al-tir'i kol asher-tom'ri e'eseh-lach ki yodeia kol-sha'ar ami ki eishet chayil at* | וְעַתָּה, בִּתִּי אַל-תִּירְאִי, כֹּל אֲשֶׁר-תֹּאמְרִי, אֶעֱשֶׂה-לָּךְ: כִּי יוֹדֵעַ כָּל-שַׁעַר עַמִּי, כִּי אֵשֶׁת חַיִל אָתְּ. | יא

12 | However, although I am a redeemer, there is another redeemer who is more closely related to you than I. | *V'atah ki amnam ki goeil anochi v'gam yeish goeil karov mimeni* | וְעַתָּה כִּי אָמְנָם, כִּי אִם גֹּאֵל אָנֹכִי; וְגַם יֵשׁ גֹּאֵל, קָרוֹב מִמֶּנִּי. | יב

13 | Stay here tonight and, when it will be morning, if he will redeem you then fine, he may redeem you. Yet, if he does not desire to redeem you, I will redeem you. I swear, as *Hashem* lives. In the meanwhile, lie down until the morning. | *Lini halailah v'hayah vaboker im-yigaleich tov yigal v'im-lo yachpotz l'ga'aleich ug'altich anochi chai-Adonai shichvi ad-haboker* | לִינִי הַלַּיְלָה, וְהָיָה בַבֹּקֶר אִם-יִגְאָלֵךְ טוֹב יִגְאָל, וְאִם-לֹא יַחְפֹּץ לְגָאֳלֵךְ וּגְאַלְתִּיךְ אָנֹכִי, חַי-יְהוָה; שִׁכְבִי, עַד-הַבֹּקֶר. | יג

14

So she slept at his feet until the morning. She got up before one man could recognize another for he had said, "Let no man know that the woman came to the threshing floor."

Vatishkav marg'lotav ad-haboker vatakom b'terem yakir ish et-rei'eihu vayomer al-yivada ki-va'ah ha'ishah hagoren

וַתִּשְׁכַּב מַרְגְּלוֹתָו, עַד-הַבֹּקֶר, וַתָּקׇם, בטרום (בְּטֶרֶם) יַכִּיר אִישׁ אֶת-רֵעֵהוּ; וַיֹּאמֶר, אַל-יִוָּדַע, כִּי-בָאָה הָאִשָּׁה, הַגֹּרֶן. יד

15

He said, "Bring me the cloth wrap that is upon you, but hold onto it." She took hold of it, and he measured six measures of barley. He placed it on her and then went to the city.

Vayomer havi hamitpachat asher-alayich v'echezi-vah vatochez bah vayamod sheish-s'orim vayaset aleha vayavo ha'ir

וַיֹּאמֶר, הָבִי הַמִּטְפַּחַת אֲשֶׁר-עָלַיִךְ וְאֶחֳזִי-בָהּ-- וַתֹּאחֶז בָּהּ; וַיָּמׇד שֵׁשׁ-שְׂעֹרִים וַיָּשֶׁת עָלֶיהָ, וַיָּבֹא הָעִיר. טו

16

She came to her mother-in-law, who said, "Who are you, my daughter?", and she told her all that the man had done for her.

Vatavo el-chamotah vatomer mi-at biti vataged-lah eit kol-asher asah-lah ha'ish

וַתָּבוֹא, אֶל-חֲמוֹתָהּ, וַתֹּאמֶר, מִי-אַתְּ בִּתִּי; וַתַּגֶּד-לָהּ--אֵת כָּל-אֲשֶׁר עָשָׂה-לָהּ, הָאִישׁ. טז

17

And *Rut* said, "He gave me these six measures of barley since he said to me, 'do not come to your mother-in-law in a state of lacking.'"

Vatomer sheish-has'orim ha'eileh natan li ki amar aylai al-tavo'i reikam el-chamotayich

וַתֹּאמֶר, שֵׁשׁ-הַשְּׂעֹרִים הָאֵלֶּה נָתַן לִי: כִּי אָמַר (אֵלַי), אַל-תָּבוֹאִי רֵיקָם אֶל-חֲמוֹתֵךְ. יז

Naomi replied to *Rut*, "Remain here, my daughter, until you know how the matter will turn out, since the man will not stop unless he settles the matter today."

Vatomer sh'vi biti ad asher teid'in eich yipol davar ki lo yishkot ha'ish ki-im-kilah hadavar hayom.

וַתֹּאמֶר, שְׁבִי בִתִּי, עַד אֲשֶׁר תֵּדְעִין, אֵיךְ יִפֹּל דָּבָר: כִּי לֹא יִשְׁקֹט הָאִישׁ, כִּי-אִם-כִּלָּה הַדָּבָר הַיּוֹם.

יח

4

ד

Boaz went up to the gate and sat there, and behold, the redeemer about whom *Boaz* had spoken passed by. He said, "Turn around and sit, *Ploni Almoni*." So, he turned and sat.

u'Boaz alah hasha'ar vayeishev sham v'hineih hag'oel avar asher diber-Boaz vayomer surah sh'vah-po p'loni almoni vayaser vayeisheiv

וּבֹעַז עָלָה הַשַּׁעַר, וַיֵּשֶׁב שָׁם, וְהִנֵּה הַגֹּאֵל עֹבֵר אֲשֶׁר דִּבֶּר-בֹּעַז, וַיֹּאמֶר סוּרָה שְׁבָה-פֹּה פְּלֹנִי אַלְמֹנִי; וַיָּסַר, וַיֵּשֵׁב.

א

Boaz then took ten men from the elders of the city and said to them, "Sit here," and they sat.

vayikach asarah anashim miziknei ha'ir vayomer sh'vu-po vayeish'vu

וַיִּקַּח עֲשָׂרָה אֲנָשִׁים, מִזִּקְנֵי הָעִיר--וַיֹּאמֶר שְׁבוּ-פֹּה; וַיֵּשֵׁבוּ.

ב

Boaz said to the redeemer, "The portion of the field that belonged to our brother *Elimelech* is being sold by *Naomi*, who has returned from the fields of Moab.

vayomer lag'oeil chelkat hasadeh asher l'achinu leElimelech mach'rah Naomi hashavah mis'dei Moav

וַיֹּאמֶר, לַגֹּאֵל, חֶלְקַת הַשָּׂדֶה, אֲשֶׁר לְאָחִינוּ לֶאֱלִימֶלֶךְ: מָכְרָה נָעֳמִי, הַשָּׁבָה מִשְּׂדֵה מוֹאָב.

ג

4

I have said that I will make it known to you, and offer you to purchase it in the presence of those sitting here and in the presence of the elders of my nation. If you wish to redeem it, redeem it. However, if you do not wish to redeem it tell me so that I will know, for there is no one else to redeem it besides you and, following you, me." He said, "I will redeem it."

va'ani amarti egleh ozn'cha leimor k'neih neged hayosh'vim v'neged ziknei ami im-tigal g'al v'im-lo yigal hagidah li v'eid'ah ki ein zulat'cha ligol va'anochi acharecha vayomer anochi eg'al

וַאֲנִי אָמַרְתִּי אֶגְלֶה אָזְנְךָ לֵאמֹר, קְנֵה נֶגֶד הַיֹּשְׁבִים וְנֶגֶד זִקְנֵי עַמִּי--אִם-תִּגְאַל גְּאָל, וְאִם-לֹא יִגְאַל הַגִּידָה לִּי ואדע (וְאֵדְעָה) כִּי אֵין זוּלָתְךָ לִגְאוֹל וְאָנֹכִי אַחֲרֶיךָ; וַיֹּאמֶר, אָנֹכִי אֶגְאָל. ד

5

Boaz then replied, "On the day that you purchase the field from *Naomi* and from *Rut* the Moabite, the wife of the deceased, you are also acquiring *Rut* in marriage in order to preserve the name of the deceased over his inheritance.

vayomer Boaz b'yom-k'not'cha hasadeh miyad Naomi umei'eit Rut haMoaviyah eishet-hameit kanita l'hakim sheim-hameit al-nachalato

וַיֹּאמֶר בֹּעַז, בְּיוֹם-קְנוֹתְךָ הַשָּׂדֶה מִיַּד נָעֳמִי; וּמֵאֵת רוּת הַמּוֹאֲבִיָּה אֵשֶׁת-הַמֵּת, קָנִיתִי (קָנִיתָ)--לְהָקִים שֵׁם-הַמֵּת, עַל-נַחֲלָתוֹ. ה

6 The redeemer responded, "If so, I am not able to redeem the field for myself, lest I destroy my own family legacy. You may redeem that which was my right to redeem for yourself, for I am not able to redeem it."

vayomer hag'oel lo uchal lig'al li pen-ashchit et-nachalati g'al-l'cha atah et-g'ulati ki lo-uchal lig'ol

וַיֹּאמֶר הַגֹּאֵל, לֹא א וּכַל לִגְאוֹל- (לִגְאָל-) לִי-פֶּן-אַשְׁחִית, אֶת-נַחֲלָתִי; גְּאַל-לְךָ אַתָּה אֶת-גְּאֻלָּתִי, כִּי לֹא-אוּ כַל לִגְאֹל.

ו

7 Now, this was originally the practice in *Yisrael* to effect every transaction in matters of redemption and exchanges: One would remove his shoe, and give it to the other party, which was the indication of the transaction's completion according to the practice of *Yisrael*.

v'zot l'fanim b'Yisrael al-hag'ulah v'al-hat'murah l'kayeim kol-davar shalaf ish na'alo v'natan l'rei'eihu v'zot hat'udah b'Yisrael

וְזֹאת לְפָנִים בְּיִשְׂרָאֵל עַל-הַגְּאֻלָּה וְעַל-הַתְּמ וּרָה, לְקַיֵּם כָּל-דָּבָר, שָׁלַף אִישׁ נַעֲלוֹ, וְנָתַן לְרֵעֵהוּ; וְזֹאת הַתְּעוּ דָה, בְּיִשְׂרָאֵל.

ז

8 The redeemer said to *Boaz*, "Acquire for yourself," and he [*Boaz*] removed his shoe.

vayomer hagoeil l'Voaz k'neih-lach vayishlof na'alo

וַיֹּאמֶר הַגֹּאֵל לְבֹעַז, קְנֵה-לָךְ; וַיִּשְׁלֹף, נַעֲלוֹ.

ח

9

Boaz then said to the elders and all of the people present "You are witnesses today that I have acquired all that belonged to *Elimelech* and all that belonged to *Kilyon* and *Machlon*, from *Naomi*.

vayomer Boaz laz'keinim v'chol-ha'am eidim atem hayom ki kaniti et-kol-asher le'Elimelech v'eit kol-asher l'Chilyon u'Machlon miyad Naomi

וַיֹּאמֶר בֹּעַז לַזְּקֵנִים וְכָל-הָעָם, עֵדִים אַתֶּם הַיּוֹם, כִּי קָנִיתִי אֶת-כָּל-אֲשֶׁר לֶאֱלִימֶלֶךְ, וְאֵת כָּל-אֲשֶׁר לְכִלְיוֹן וּמַחְלוֹן--מִיַּד, נָעֳמִי.

ט

10

And I have also acquired *Rut* the Moabite, the wife of *Machlon*, as a wife, in order to preserve the name of the deceased over his inheritance, and so that his name will not be lost from among his brothers and the entrance to his place. You are, today, my witnesses."

v'gam et-Rut haMoaviyah eishet Machlon kaniti li l'ishah l'hakim sheim-hameit al-nachalato v'lo-yikareit sheim-hameit mei'im echav umisha'ar m'komo eidim atem hayom

וְגַם אֶת-רוּת הַמֹּאֲבִיָּה אֵשֶׁת מַחְלוֹן קָנִיתִי לִי לְאִשָּׁה, לְהָקִים שֵׁם-הַמֵּת עַל-נַחֲלָתוֹ, וְלֹא-יִכָּרֵת שֵׁם-הַמֵּת מֵעִם אֶחָיו, וּמִשַּׁעַר מְקוֹמוֹ: עֵדִים אַתֶּם, הַיּוֹם.

י

11

All of the people that were in the entrance to the city and the elders said, "We are witnesses. May *Hashem* enable the woman who is coming into your house to be like *Rachel* and like *Leah*, both of whom built the House of *Yisrael*. May you be successful in *Efrat* and may you perpetuate your name in *Beit Lechem*.

vayom'ru kol-ha'am asher-basha'ar v'haz'kenim eidim yitein Adonai et-ha'ishah haba'ah el-beitecha k'Rachel uchLeah asher banu sh'teihem et-beit Yisrael va'aseih-chayil b'Efratah ukra-sheim b'Veit Lachem

וַיֹּאמְרוּ כָּל-הָעָם אֲשֶׁר-בַּשַּׁעַר, וְהַזְּקֵנִים-עֵדִים; יִתֵּן יְהוָה אֶת-הָאִשָּׁה הַבָּאָה אֶל-בֵּיתֶךָ, כְּרָחֵל וּכְלֵאָה אֲשֶׁר בָּנוּ שְׁתֵּיהֶם אֶת-בֵּית יִשְׂרָאֵל, וַעֲשֵׂה-חַיִל בְּאֶפְרָתָה, וּקְרָא-שֵׁם בְּבֵית לָחֶם.

יא

12 May your house be like the house of *Peretz*, whom *Tamar* bore to *Yehuda*, through the child that *Hashem* will bestow upon you from this young woman."

vihi veit'cha k'veit Peretz asher-yal'dah Tamar liYehudah min-hazera asher yiten Adonai l'cha min-hana'arah hazot

וִיהִי בֵיתְךָ כְּבֵית פֶּרֶץ, אֲשֶׁר-יָלְדָה תָמָר לִיה וּדָה--מִן-הַזֶּרַע, אֲשֶׁר יִתֵּן יְהוָה לְךָ, מִן-הַנַּעֲרָה, הַזֹּאת. יב

13 *Boaz* then took *Rut* and she became his wife. He came to her and *Hashem* enabled her to conceive, and she gave birth to a son.

vayikach Boaz et-Rut vat'hi-lo l'ishah vayavo eileha vayitein Adonai lah heirayon vateiled bein

וַיִּקַּח בֹּעַז אֶת-רוּת וַתְּהִי-לוֹ לְאִשָּׁה, וַיָּבֹא אֵלֶיהָ; וַיִּתֵּן יְהוָה לָהּ הֵרָיוֹן, וַתֵּלֶד בֵּן. יג

14 The local women then said to *Naomi*, "Blessed is *Hashem*, who has not withheld a redeemer from you today, and his name will be called in *Yisrael.*

vatomarnah hanashim el-Naomi baruch Adonai asher lo hishbit lach go'eil hayom v'yikarei sh'mo biYisrael

וַתֹּאמַרְנָה הַנָּשִׁים, אֶל-נָעֳמִי, בָּרוּךְ יְהוָה, אֲשֶׁר לֹא הִשְׁבִּית לָךְ גֹּאֵל הַיּוֹם; וְיִקָּרֵא שְׁמ ו, בְּיִשְׂרָאֵל. יד

15 He will be one who returns your soul and supports you in your senior years, for your daughter-in-law, who loves you, has given birth to him. She is better to you than seven sons."

v'hayah lakh l'meishiv nefesh ulchalkeil et-seivateich ki chalateich asher-aheivatech y'ladatu asher-hi tovah lach mishivah banim

וְהָיָה לָךְ לְמֵשִׁיב נֶפֶשׁ, וּלְכַלְכֵּל אֶת-שֵׂיבָתֵךְ: כִּי כַלָּתֵךְ אֲשֶׁר-אֲהֵבַתֶךְ, יְלָדַתּוּ, אֲשֶׁר-הִיא טוֹבָה לָךְ, מִשִּׁבְעָה בָּנִים. טו

| 16 | *Naomi* took the boy and she drew him towards her heart, and she took care of him. | *vatikach Naomi et-hayeled vatishiteihu v'cheikah vat'hi-lo l'omenet* | וַתִּקַּח נָעֳמִי אֶת-הַיֶּלֶד וַתְּשִׁתֵהוּ בְחֵיקָהּ, וַתְּהִי-לוֹ לְאֹמֶנֶת. | טז |

| 17 | And the neighbors declared that it was as though a son had been born to *Naomi*, and they called him *Oved*. He is the father of *Yishai*, who was the father of *David*. | *Vatikrenah lo hash'cheinot sheim leimor yulad-bein l'Naomi vatikrenah sh'mo Oveid hu avi-Yishai avi-David {P}* | וַתִּקְרֶאנָה לוֹ הַשְּׁכֵנוֹת שֵׁם לֵאמֹר, יֻלַּד-בֵּן לְנָעֳמִי; וַתִּקְרֶאנָה שְׁמוֹ עוֹבֵד, הוּא אֲבִי-יִשַׁי אֲבִי דָוִד. | יז |

| 18 | These are the generations of *Peretz*: *Peretz* fathered *Chetzron*. | *V'eileh tol'dot Paretz, Peretz holid et-Chetzron* | וְאֵלֶּה תּוֹלְדוֹת פָּרֶץ, פֶּרֶץ הוֹלִיד אֶת-חֶצְרוֹן. | יח |

| 19 | *Chetzron* fathered *Ram*, and *Ram* fathered *Aminadav*. | *V'Chetzron holid et-Ram v'Ram holid et-Aminadav* | וְחֶצְרוֹן הוֹלִיד אֶת-רָם, וְרָם הוֹלִיד אֶת-עַמִּינָדָב. | יט |

| 20 | *Aminadav* fathered *Nachshon*, and *Nachshon* fathered *Salma*. | *v'Aminadav holid et-Nachshon v'Nachshon holid et-Salma* | וְעַמִּינָדָב הוֹלִיד אֶת-נַחְשׁוֹן, וְנַחְשׁוֹן הוֹלִיד אֶת-שַׂלְמָה. | כ |

| 21 | *Salma* fathered *Boaz*, and *Boaz* fathered *Oved*. | *V'Salmon holid et-Boaz uVoaz holid et-Oveid* | וְשַׂלְמוֹן הוֹלִיד אֶת-בֹּעַז, וּבֹעַז הוֹלִיד אֶת-עוֹבֵד. | כא |

| 22 | *Oved* fathered *Yishai*, and *Yishai* fathered *David*. | *V'Oveid holid et-Yishai v'Yishai holid et-David* | וְעֹבֵד הוֹלִיד אֶת-יִשַׁי, וְיִשַׁי הוֹלִיד אֶת-דָּוִד. | כב |

Rabbi Leo's Eulogy for Rina and Maia

Rabbis, Ministers, Members of the Knesset, Mayor Revivi, Social Worker Anat, family and friends. I know my darling wife Lucy would have asked me to state, from the beginning, that these words are from the two of us. Tonight, as ever, the sentiments are from her, she is my CEO and I'm just the scribe.

Firstly, thank you from the bottom of our hearts for your warmth, your kindness and your love. Never have we ever seen such an outpouring of love. And thank you to everyone who has helped in every possible way, I've not had to do anything and everything has been done. All of you are righteous, you are all a miracle! Rabbi Akiva Tatz once taught me a question asked in the Talmud: if Siamese twins, two babies conjoined at the hip or at the head, are born, are they considered to be one person or two separate people? The Sages explain that you must perform the following test: if you hurt one of the bodies and the other side feels the pain, then the Siamese twins are considered one person. Today the Jewish people have proven that we are one, that we are a united people.

When a simple, quiet family in Efrat is devastated, the whole country hurts. And when a family in Tel Aviv is devastated, the whole country hurts. There is no greater proof of our unity. *Am Yisrael Chai*, the people of Israel live! We know this. We have *always* known this. We have been marching through the streets of Jerusalem and Tel Aviv with Israeli flags arguing over the issue of judicial reform. Let's be honest, most of us have no idea what any of this means. But in three weeks' time on *Yom HaZikaron* (Israel's Memorial Day) and *Yom Ha'Atzmaut* (Israel's Independence Day), we will once again be marching, side by side, carrying our Israeli flags, left wing next to right-wing, religious next to secular, united against the real threat - the threat of pure evil, the threat of the Islamic

55

terrorist funded by Iran, Hamas and Hezbollah, the terrorist with a Kalashnikov rifle who doesn't care whether you're from Efrat or Tel Aviv, London or Italy, and who's prepared to destroy your children's lives in an instant. *Then* we will march as one. *Am Yisrael Chai!*

Some people have asked me, how can you have such faith in God's continued goodness? Please God, it should last more than just today. And I have told them that I have listened to almost all of Rabbi Efrem Goldberg's classes on faith, available online on yutorah.org, in which he repeats over and over again that there is one main formula for faith. Always focus on what you *do* have and not on what you do *not*. I still have three wonderful children, Keren, Tali and Yehuda, and a wonderful wife Lucy (Leah bat Tzipora), may she, please God, soon come out of her coma [ed. note: sadly, Lucy died of her injuries a few days later]. And Maia and Rina, who lie before us, *you* are now part of us all, forever. If the Jewish people would look at what we *have*, and not at what we do *not*, we would realize that we still are a united people, united against our common enemy. We are the forces of good fighting the forces of evil. And we will always prevail! *Am Yisrael Chai!*

The Talmud tells the story of the wife of Rabbi Meir, who did not want to disturb his *Shabbat* afternoon class to tell him that their two sons had just died from a deadly virus. After *Shabbat*, she broke the news of their death by asking him the question: "Before *Shabbat* someone brought me a precious gift. Now they have come and want to take it back. Should I return the gift or not?" How will I explain to Lucy what has happened to our two precious gifts, Maia and Rina, when she wakes up from her coma?

My beautiful, perfect, special Maia - we named you "Maia," "God's water," and you were a friend to so many people, flowing between so many different groups. Every week, you were out on Friday night with one group of friends, with another group in our lounge on *Shabbat* afternoon and a third visit to a close friend on Saturday night. Maia, at your *Bat Mitzvah* (Jewish coming-of-age ceremony) just eight short years ago, we tried to find a biblical character to compare you to. Rachel, Esther, Rebecca? Then we realized that you were most like the Matriarch Sarah since, in your twelve years, you moved to Israel at the age of two, left at age six and came back at age eleven - just like the biblical Sarah, who also entered and left Israel twice. Sadly the comparison does not stop there. Sarah was buried in *Ma'arat HaMachpela* (The Cave of the Patriarchs), the cave in Hebron where each of the forefathers was buried along with their spouse in pairs. And Maia, today, you and Rina will also be buried in a double grave.

Maia, you wanted to volunteer for another year of national service where you could really make a difference for Israel. But Mummy and I wanted you to start your studies and maybe meet a special boy. But you insisted that girls like you always do two years of volunteering. We were waiting to see where you would serve. You were always an angel. And now you will always be our guardian angel.

My beautiful darling Rina, you were such a great student, such a great friend, such a great youth leader. You were so responsible. If the Ezra youth club needed to clean up on a Friday morning and you were the only one who turned up to help, you would do it single-handedly for three hours. People loved you and always knew they could depend on you. Less than two weeks ago, twenty of your girls slept over in our home with your co-youth-leader, Adi. Mummy and I had to find somewhere else to spend that night. The girls made so much noise but had so much fun.

Rina Bina, you were considering joining the army in two years' time, after a year of studying in seminary, possibly to work in intelligence. You dreamt of traveling the world. And now you are traveling to heaven. You, too, are an angel and I know you are currently organizing God's youth club in heaven.

In the Torah reading for the *Shabbat* of Passover, which we read yesterday, Moses asks God to see His face. God explains to Moses: "You shall see My back, but My face shall not be seen" (Exodus 33:23). Rabbi Lord Jonathan Sacks explained that Moses was asking God: "Show me why bad things happen to good people!" but God answers: "You will never know, except, possibly, by looking back from the distant future." The message is: we can never understand God's will.

But this past *Shabbat* we also read a passage from Ezekiel about the valley of dry bones. We read of bones in the valley - perhaps the Jordan Valley, where you were both so suddenly taken away from us - which come back to life. Maia and Rina - you, too, are coming back to life. You are two flames that have not gone out. Your flames have added to our flames and are strengthening them, bringing more and more light to the world through every one of us. *Am Yisrael Chai!*

Today, we celebrate the festival of Passover when the Jewish people left Egypt and crossed the Red Sea, a process that took just one week. But it was not easy sailing. After three days, God told the people: "Turn back and encamp before *Pi-hahiroth*, between *Migdol* and the sea... And Pharaoh will say of the children of Israel: They are entangled in the land, the wilderness hath shut them in" (Exodus 14:2-3). *Pi HaCherut* is *Pitom*, the very place they were slaves for 210 years. God sent them straight back into the hands of Pharaoh! They had to come out a second time. Two exoduses - yes, we actually left Egypt *twice*! The message is that the journey to redemption is a slow one. Three steps forward and two steps back. And Maia and Rina, with your loss, our world has taken two steps back.

It is customary in Israel to ask forgiveness from the departed at the funeral: Rina and Maia, if any of us here have ever hurt your feelings or treated you without the respect that you deserved, please forgive us. We would never have done that intentionally. Maia and Rina, you have inspired us, you have loved us, and, in turn, we will continue to love both of you, forever. May your souls be bound in the bond of eternal life and may we, and no one else in the world, ever know so much sorrow. Amen.

Rabbi Leo's Eulogy for his wife Lucy

Lucy, you wanted me to give a special speech at your 50th birthday. And now this. Lucy, you were a great companion for anyone. But for me, you were my best friend, and I yours. We literally traveled the world together, we made *aliyah* to Israel together and built a new life for ourselves in the promised land. You would frequently say that you couldn't imagine living anywhere else. Nor could I. Even now. Especially now.

What a warm embrace we have felt from the people of Efrat, Gush Etzion, Israel and worldwide. During the COVID pandemic we spent so much time together. During lockdowns, we would sneak down Highway 60 which was completely empty and head off to the Dead Sea, where we hiked every riverbed. That was your passion and you made it mine. So much so that for my 50th birthday last year you took me to the Lower Darga walk, where we climbed down 20 dangerous waterfalls with a 30-meter rope. That day at Darga there was a group of fit Israeli soldiers and us. You were proud of the achievement but said you would never ever do it again.

When COVID ended, we made a decision: we would reduce our working week to four days and go hiking on Thursdays with one another. And so we did. Every week for the last two and a half years. Recently, I started feeling a little guilty for taking so much time off of work and would prepare for my math class for a few hours on Thursday afternoon. Now, I wish I'd taken off every Sunday, Monday, Tuesday and Wednesday too.

You were so generous: you trained to be a new mother counselor and visited a new mother and baby in Efrat every week to give her support. You mentored a new teacher in Jerusalem, zooming with him weekly to help him learn the ropes. You organized the *Shabbat* class for women in our neighborhood, finding speakers and locations.

We spent years together as a rabbinic couple in Hendon and Radlett from 2004 to 2014. Those were wonderful years when we also had much time for one another. I say "rabbinic couple" because you were the main event and I was just the occasional speaker. You brought people together in our home, arranging social events for festivals, bouncy castles for the kids on Chanukah, and hosting twenty people around our Shabbat table most weeks.

Speaking of Shabbat meals, your Friday night chicken soup recipe was a secret, unknown even to me. I was allowed to help on any dish except for the chicken soup. But last Shabbat you were so busy grading national English oral proficiency tests that you WhatsApped me the recipe. Now I will have to make the chicken soup alone - but at least it will be like yours.

You were an amazing mother. You described yourself as the CEO of the family and me as the COO. The kids had to participate in the home - laundry, cooking, washing up. You would tell me what you wanted the kids to do and I would be the one to manage them. That way, you thought, they would resent me and not you for making them work! The problem was that they knew I didn't have a clue as to what needed to be done and that the tasks ultimately came from you. You thought that this would make the kids love you less. On the contrary, because you got them to help, they loved you more.

You were an excellent English teacher. You began your training when we arrived back in Israel in 2014, and you worked while you studied. You started off in some difficult schools with some difficult students, and at times I wanted to tell you just to quit. Then you found your place, and became the most inspiring of teachers. You used technology, you played games, you engaged the kids. You inspired me and many others to take up teaching. You were magnetic. You believed that the shortage of English teachers in Israel at the moment was a perfect opportunity for Anglos to make *aliyah*. Today, I understand, you can start teaching English and learn how to teach English, while getting a decent salary from day one. You dreamt of a wave of English Jews, including our families, coming to live in Israel.

You cared about all of us, writing special notes for us, baking gluten-free cakes, and making delicious vegetarian food - veggie lasagna, veggie meatballs and rice, and we would come home from a day at work or school and find it sitting on the counter with a little note explaining how to heat it up.

At the hospital yesterday, I saw a young couple with a few young children at the top of the escalators. They were getting a little annoyed with the children who were arguing with one another. I wanted to tell them to enjoy every moment because you never know what tomorrow will bring.

Lucy, I don't think I would have said this at your 50th, but it's appropriate now. You improved yourself throughout your life. I fell in love with you during a Shavuot all-night learning program that you had put together for Oxford University Jewish Society. The Rabbi had to cancel at the last minute and you stepped up to arrange students to speak from 10 pm through to 5 am. You said you fell in love with me because the speakers only had 20 minutes of content for each hour slot, but I asked so many questions that each class dragged on for an hour.

The next day we played bridge at my friend's room. The two of us were pitted against two students studying for a PhD in math. We won. I overbid, you underbid, and together we somehow got it right. After 24 hours I came back to London and told my elderly grandmother that I'd met the girl I was to marry. You were then 21 and I was 23, but you spent a year in Japan so it took two more years to happen. Since then, I have continued to overbid - I was the one who stood up in the synagogue and spoke and got the glory. You continued to underbid - you were the one who did all the hard work, modestly, and received less acclaim. But the strength for everything I did in my life came from you. From where will that strength come now?

Your favorite programs that we watched on the computer in bed at night were Bake Off, MasterChef, Pottery Throwdown and Sewing Bee. These shows are all about people doing things they are passionate about and doing them extremely well. We both loved the passion that amateurs had for their hobbies - cooking, pottery, sewing. When we see people with passion, their enthusiasm rubs off on us. In the words of our Sages: "What comes from the heart speaks to the heart." You were so passionate about Maia, Keren, Tali, Rina, and Yehuda, and you shared your passions with them. Your passion for life has rubbed off on them and I know that will help us pull through this.

In the Song of Songs that we read each Friday before *Shabbat*, the lover tries to contact his bride, knocking on her door. "*Kol dodi dofeki,*" "My beloved is knocking." She really wants to greet him, but it takes her time to organize herself. By the time she gets to the door, he has left, "*Dodi chamak avar,*" "My beloved has slipped away." She thinks that he thinks she no longer loves him. But Lucy, I will continue to knock and to wait and I will never take your absence as a sign that our love has burnt out.

In King Solomon's "Woman of Valor" (Proverbs 31:10-31) that we sang each Friday night around our table and by your bedside yesterday together, it states: "Her children rise and acclaim her and her husband praises her" (Proverbs 31:28). Lucy, I am sorry that in your lifetime we did not say these things enough, though you wouldn't have even allowed us to. Why did it take until now for us to praise you?

You were airlifted from the murder scene. I can't imagine the pain, physical and mental, if you were conscious in any way for that journey. On Sunday I talked about looking at the good. Lucy, I have a choice. I could lament over the next 25 years of marriage that I have lost. But I can also feel blessed to have had 25 years of a beautiful marriage with you. By Friday your life was at its peak. You had really got your seven F's in order: Friends, Family, Fitness, Faith, Function, Finances and Flame.

When we occasionally had an evening out for dinner together, we would go through them all, each of us separately, and score how our life was progressing against these seven important dimensions. We knew that we could never be perfect at all seven at once, since spending more time with family means spending less time with friends and spending more time at work means less time for one another. But precisely last week, you seemed at complete balance for the first time. Not me. But you. Bizarre.

Non-Jewish friends of mine have asked why we customarily place simple stones on the graves of our loved ones when we visit, instead of expensive flowers. I don't know the official answer, but my father gave me some of his wisdom once and it seems to be spot on. He told me that you must treat someone well while they are alive so that when they are no longer here, you feel no regrets. You mustn't feel: "I wish I'd just told her..." If you do this, you don't need to buy expensive flowers for the grave, and can spend the money on someone who is alive or give it to charity. The stone is enough to show you care. Lucy, I know you know I love you. I know you know we all love you. Stones today will be enough.

You didn't always like your Hebrew name, Leah. Leah was the less loved wife of Jacob, who preferred Rachel. Why did you have to be named after the second best? But then you realized that by giving Joseph preferential treatment, Jacob and Rachel caused much animosity among the family. Leah was far more even-handed with her children, who all felt her love equally. Ultimately, the Messiah will come from the tribe of Judah, Leah's son, and not from Rachel. And Leah, who was second to Rachel in her lifetime, was buried in the double grave with Jacob in our holy city of Hebron. Like Leah, we too will be buried in a double grave, but our double grave will soon be half full next to our girls, fifty years too early.

Lucy, did we fight? Sure we fought. And in front of the kids. You felt that was good. That they should know that in a relationship fighting is natural. It's part of growing together. God forbid the children should marry and break up after their first major argument because they felt it wasn't working. We always tried to keep to the rules of the Talmud and make up before we went to sleep at night. The logic was that people often die in their sleep, so make up with each other while you still can.

On *Seder* night, the first night of Passover, I quoted David Sacks's spotify podcast. Sacks, previously a script writer for the Simpsons and now an inspiring returnee to traditional Judaism, lamented with his excellent command of English about the way we misuse many words in our speech. We say, "I need a new car," "I need a new dress," "I need a new phone." But he asks us to think about what we have. "I have a close family," "I have a loving wife," "I have a warm community." And then he says to change the word 'have' for the word 'need' and the word 'need' for the word 'want.' "I want a new dress - I don't need it'" "I want a new phone - I don't need it." And likewise, "I need a close family" "I need a warm community". What we have is what we need. What we say we need is only what we want. So, "Lucy, I need you back" translates to "Lucy, I want you back". And "I have three beautiful children" translates to, "I need three beautiful children." It sounds like a small change, but it really helps when you can't sleep at night. I am learning to appreciate what I have now, for we can never assume that it will be there tomorrow.

Lucy had another little discussion topic that we would regularly bring up at our Shabbat table when the kids were younger. We should have continued it. Lord Rabbi Jonathan Sacks once instructed us to ask three questions around the family table: What did you do for someone today? What did someone do for you today? What did God do for you today? Try it, it's amazing. It forces you to think about the important things in life and not the day-to-day stuff. What Rabbi Sacks called the eulogy values, not the resume values.

What did I do for someone today? Lucy, I'm eulogizing you. What did someone do for me today? The list is too long - but thank you to all of you who have been here for us. What did Hashem do for me today? He brought us to live in Israel and to make our lives here. And he gave us all of you, the Jewish people, and many non-Jewish people, who have come out in force to support us at this time.

Danja is a very good friend of Lucy, an example to us all. When COVID struck she had to quit her job as a Dutch speaking tour guide and decided to volunteer 40-80 hours a week for MADA, the Israeli ambulance service, as a driver. She was at Ein Kerem Hospital last night and posted this message that she wanted me to share:

"I hope it's ok that I'm writing. I don't know who else to tell... I am sitting in the *Chadar Leida* (the hospital birthing rooms) on a shift. We have no anesthetists. They are all in surgeries bringing life to people who will, please God, live long healthy lives. Thanks to Lucy and Leo and their beautiful, brave family. I've been crying on and off since I came to work. But I'm not useless. I have the power to help the women in pain cope. I can pray for the women of Israel, for the mothers and fathers and sisters and brothers and friends who need God's help more than ever. For all of Israel. To bring us back. To not feel lost. To feel God's power and admit we are powerless to control it all. And to give it up to Him. With love and hope and faith. For this I pray tonight in the *Chadar Leida*, at the birthing rooms with no anesthetists."

Thank you to everyone who is pouring in love. Dees Day - if nothing else, it was a tremendous comfort to us when I woke up in the middle of the night and saw Facebook, with so many smiling faces with Israeli flags from all over the world.

Mayor Oded Revivi, the Efrat that you have helped to create is giving us incredible strength. When we left our home and traveled through the streets of Efrat and there were literally thousands of people waving flags as we passed by, we felt like the royal family. But then we realized that no royal family would ever get such a warm greeting. The thousands of social media posts of families with Israeli flags helped thousands of people who live outside of Efrat get a taste of the level of warmth that we have inside our small but growing community.

We are blessed to be part of this thriving city and we are blessed to be part of the people of Israel! We are blessed to be part of a humanity that is beginning to wake up and recognize its soul. Thank you for your love. I never was that sort of person, Lucy was. I don't deserve it, but she does. Maybe I am getting this in her merit.

My son Yehuda said yesterday that we should not ask "*Lama*," "Why?," but rather "*Le'ma?*," "For what?" We can never say "Why us? Why Lucy? Why Rina? Why Maia?" But perhaps we can say "For what?," and maybe we can answer, "Why now?"

This week of Passover is the week of leaving slavery and learning to be free. Did this awesome event unleash a power? Is there a latent power in humanity that transcends the borders of countries, religion and politics? In an era where truth is defined by the number of likes you receive on social media, is there a higher truth, Something that we can all sense? Were we all born with a built in moral navigational system, but never taught how to use it? Could it be that there is a new awareness growing in humanity that we are all connected? Could it be that since we all came from the same spark that we all have the same moment of creation? That we are all one? Is there a higher truth than the one we read in our algorithmically generated newsfeeds? Could the timeless knowledge of our ancestors still have something to teach us so many thousands of years later? Were there things that they knew but that we have forgotten, and now need to remember?

Thousands of people have contacted me in the past few days and I thank you all. But if people have the time to contact me in their busy schedules, then how many of us also have the time to do one more thing for someone else, for someone who is alive, who would appreciate it even more?

I want to conclude; you've been here long enough. I wondered if I were to ask Lucy to make a blessing for all of us, what would she say? I think she would say:

Forgive, for when you hold grudges it only hurts you.

Apologize, even if it's not your fault.. Don't get upset for too long. If in five years' time it's not going to be a big deal then it does not deserve more than five minutes of your time now.

Be *passionate* about what you do. If you're not, then change what you do. The first commandment discussed in the *Shulchan Aruch* [a classic Jewish book about the commandments] is to "Rise like a lion." How can we do this? Surely you can't be commanded to rise like a lion?! I think it must mean that you must find something you're passionate about so that you *want* to jump out of bed in the mornings to do it. If you don't want to jump out of bed, then change your occupation. You don't have to be the best. You have to give it your best.

Explore - grow older if you are so fortunate, but never grow up. There should always be a wonder in everything.

Love all your children equally. Love is something that is not a zero sum game - the more you share the more you have.

Lucy you shared your love and you created so much love in return. Nothing will ever replace you, you are part of my soul. Your lessons live on in Keren, Tali and Yehuda and in me. Your light has traveled across all of humanity in an instant. You held on so we could honor you individually and give you a unique send off for a unique soul. A soul that has changed and will continue to change many lives. May your soul be bound up in the bond of everlasting life, amen.

Keren Dee's Eulogy for her Mum

Yesterday, at Maia and Rina's grave, I closed my eyes and prayed that you would wake up so that we wouldn't have to go through this pain twice. What if mom doesn't wake up? I've already lost sisters, I can't lose her too!

My heart is already so full of sorrow that I am paralyzed with pain. To lose a mother is like losing a life. It is impossible to move forward from here. God, what else do you want to take from me?? I don't want to forget. Now I will have to take on two positions at home and for this no one has prepared me.

We went on a journey together, we worked on our relationship and built it until we became the best of friends and we enjoyed being together. You taught me so much without me realizing it. You took care of me in every way possible. You were the one in our family holding us together like glue. No one else can tell me what to do, or put me in my place, besides you. Everyone else will move on, and only we will be left behind with this hole that can never be filled.

Mom, you would always sing "*Hamalach Hagoel,*" "The angel who has redeemed me from evil," (Genesis 48:16), before we went to bed. When we were little, you said the "*Modeh Ani,*" the morning prayer, with us in the morning. I will try to pass these traditions on to our children. Even with a thousand words, I won't be able to sum you up, I won't even try, it's impossible, you are my mother, that's all!

From now on I will have to light the Shabbat candles. Mom, you always told me that you are waiting for grandchildren and to become a grandmother. Now in life they will never get to know what kind of mother you were, but I promise that we will tell them everything. You told me that even if I marry a *Sabra,* a native Israeli, you will take on the responsibility to teach my children English and to read them books in English. Who will accompany me to the *Chuppah* (the marriage canopy)?

I would always look forward to the Shabbat songs that all us girls would sing together on Friday night. But now it will be just me and Tali; from five girls we have gone down to two.

As everyone knows there is nothing better than Mum's food. Everything I know about cooking is thanks to you, and everyone always says that I cook delicious food.

I see the family photo by your bed and remember that we are no more. At every event we went to, I always knew that I would look for your face in the crowd and that you would be there. You made sure that we were close. There were always family events and you made sure everyone came; you were the reason we are so close.

You were shot twice and you fought for your life. You have always been a strong woman, from your childhood that was not simple, until the very last moment. Whenever you would take me to workout and we would get in shape together with all the older women, you were proud that you brought me.

Last night, I went to sleep in Rina's bed, in Tali's room. I can't believe that Daddy is now sleeping alone. I really didn't want to be here again. After all the prayers, I really thought to myself that it wouldn't happen. We sang songs next to your bed on Saturday night, and you didn't wake up.

I can't go back to normal. I don't feel like saying that I'll miss you because I can't digest the fact that it's over. I don't know how to end this eulogy, because no matter how I end it, I'll never be able to include everything in it, because you can't be summed up in words.

I love you Mummy.

Keren's Eulogy for Rina

Rina, my wonderful sister.

Rinush, you wanted a good picture to post just in case, God forbid, a situation like this was to happen. But no picture is nearly good enough to express who you are. Rini, we could look at each other and immediately know what the other was thinking. We had our own telepathy. Right now you know what I'm thinking and I only hope I have the strength to know what you're thinking. I see you constantly.

Last year, we removed the wall between our rooms so we could be together. You were always there for everyone and the family was always so important to you, you'd leave notes for us and Mummy and Daddy in all kinds of places. We would chat for hours and talk about everything in the world. You'd come talk to me about *Bagruyot* (high school exams), *Snif* (youth groups), being a counselor, the army and all your plans for the future. Lately our bond became even stronger, and I wish I could talk to you more.

It was so good for me too to talk to you and hear all of your insights and how you'd see the world in such a special way. Just this past *Seder* night (the night of the first Passover meal) you said so many smart things and I'd always learned so much from you.

A sentence that really characterized you was "If I am not for myself who will be?" You would always take responsibility for things, whether it was with the new *Snif* where you'd always offer our house for staff activities because you didn't yet have a building, or how you'd always care for the girls who didn't have anyone to talk to or meet up with. You would always see the kids standing on the side and find a way to get them involved. You would offer to help long before anyone even asked. You would always stay behind to help clean up and you'd be the last to leave because that's just how you were.

Even when you were having a hard time you'd never give up. You were also so quick to help as soon as anyone asked. You were the first to get to *Snif* to help out for *Shabbat et la'asot* (a *Shabbat* dedicated to volunteering) and you were there up until the moment *Shabbat* began. You inherited this quickness from Mummy.

You'd always say that our hearts follow our actions, that by doing good we will become good people. You were a person of action, you were always doing. You had such strong values and you lived by them. You were a vegetarian because you believed in it and you always explained to people why. You knew that if we wanted to solve the climate crisis you had to do your part. You also believed in settling the land of Israel, so you volunteered with *Hashomer Hachadash* (a volunteer organization dedicated to safeguarding the land and farms in the Negev and Galilee and upholding the Zionist ideals on which Israel was founded). After a week in the school dorms, you'd go to sleep on some farm and wake up early in the morning to help a farmer. Then, when it was time to come home for *Shabbat*, you didn't want to bother our parents so you'd hitchhike and take buses to get home just in time.

"A wise person listens twice," you would always say, and explain that if you listen well the first time you already know it when it's said the second time. You had both the wisdom of the heart and the wisdom of the mind. You always understood people and their needs and you were never condescending. Everyone felt comfortable talking to you. You had so many friends from so many different places and social circles and you were the bridge between all of them. You were very successful in school and it all came to you easily. You would always say the smartest things in class.

You really wanted to invent something that could help solve the environmental crisis. You wanted to get a degree and serve in the Israeli army's Talpiot program (an elite training program for recruits who have demonstrated outstanding academic ability in the sciences and leadership potential). You wanted to help everyone with your intelligence.

Rina, I know how much you hated blood, just like Daddy. She had such a wonderful mind, and I always told her to become a doctor and invent new medicines. But she wouldn't go near blood. She didn't like blood one bit. I can't imagine what those final moments were like for you.

As your sister, I was supposed to protect you from everything, but I couldn't. I would have taken every single one of those bullets instead of you if I could, but I can't. So now I need you to protect me and be there for me.

It's *Sefirat Ha'omer* (the seven-week period between Passover and Shavuot), so we're all grieving together. I know what we have lost by losing you, and everyone who knows you understands. The world is losing so much. Please, everyone, try to be strong and good like Rina.

Rina, you always said you wanted to be more like me. No, Rina, I want to be more like you. Everyone needs to be more like you, for that way the redemption will come. I love you more than anything in the world.

Tali's Eulogy for Maia and Rina

I'm always one who tries to think about the future and be prepared for the next step, but even I could not have imagined this. I never could have prepared myself for this.

My beautiful Maia.

You're my oldest sister and, knowingly or unknowingly, I've always followed in your footsteps. Whether it was going to Neveh Chanah High School, choosing Oshri as my driving teacher, or going to Lod next year for national service. The way you talked about places and your experiences in such a bright manner and with so much excitement, how could I not?

You're my second half. We were similar both in our appearance and personality, although we never admitted it. We painted our nails the same color on Tuesday and talked about life and friends. You were able to describe my friends' personalities just from hearing my stories, without ever having met them. You'd always laugh when I told stories. We even bought the same dress for Passover and fought over who'd get to wear it first.

It was always so important to you to listen to everyone. You always asked me about my day, you'd call me from Yerucham to talk because you were always interested in my life. You always spoke to me as an equal. You'd work so hard to help your friends and organize the house before they came over to hang out. You even made desserts, special for them. You once had two hours free between meeting up with friends. I told you to rest but you went and called another friend to meet up because you wanted to see everyone.

Maia, you put your all into everything. You worked hard in school and never let yourself give in. You worked so hard doing your national service in Yerucham, giving private lessons to students who were struggling. You led a group that studied the weekly *Parsha* (Bible portion) and brought snacks for all the kids. You organized everything on your own.

You invested in your religious growth. You chose to study for a year in *midrasha* (religious seminary) and, oh, how you loved the classes! You would share the Torah you learned at our *Shabbat* table and with the students at Yerucham. The Torah really lit you up; you even learned *Daf Yomi* (daily Talmud study) with Daddy. You were so smart. You knew how to say everything in just the right way. You were a perfectionist, you made sure things would be exactly how you wanted them to be. Whether it was your beliefs, keeping the house clean, or your room, everything was exactly how it should be.

Besides all the big things, you were a funny person. You told such funny stories. When I close my eyes, I see your massive smile; I see you laughing with water spraying out of your mouth and nose! You were super honest and full of confidence, you weren't embarrassed to speak the truth. I could always trust you and get your advice.

I want to apologize, but that's pointless. We're sisters, no matter what, and I know you love me, and I love you. That's how family is.

Maia, I'll always walk on your path and I know you will guide me from above. Now that I don't have you, I have no one to show me what to do, I don't have anyone to gossip with about the classes in Lod, I don't have anyone to give me advice about boys or to laugh and joke with about having a boyfriend and getting married. I don't have your laughter, your curls, or your determination. I don't have you.

You were strong, the strongest there is, which you got from Mummy. I never saw you cry, you knew how to cope.

My friend Orit once spoke about what kind of person is worthy of admiration. Maia and Rina, you are both worthy of being admired.

The world has lost two incredible souls. We'll go home and nothing will be the same without you. The bond between sisters is the longest lasting bond there is. Even though I was only granted 17 years with you, Maia, and 15 with you, Rina, you will always be with me, on my shoulders, guiding me for the rest of my life.

I'll remember you Rina every time I say *Shir Ha'Ma'alot* (Psalm 126), and with every *Hallel* (prayer of thanksgiving said on Jewish holidays) when I say "This is God's doing; it is marvelous in our eyes" (Psalm 118:23).

Rina and Maia loved everyone. They loved leftists and secular Jews. They loved a good argument with people of different opinions, but also to find a way to agree with people and find similarities to bring everyone together with a common goal.

Rina, you'd want us to unite as a nation, so that we'd be there to support each other. You'd want us to always take the initiative and be active people who do good.

Maia, you'd want us to always laugh and be happy, to always hug each other, to be strong and committed, and to put our all into everything we do.

Thank you Maia and Rina. Thank you for protecting Mummy for us. I'm sorry we couldn't be there instead of you.

We are neither the first to suffer from this, nor will we be the last. We'll somehow get through this and help other people, just as other people are helping us. There are amazing people who, the second I called, were ready with open arms. People that helped with all the little details that we are unable to deal with on our own. People who came to our home to bring us anything we were missing and people who showed up at the hospital, seconds before *Shabbat*, to bring us cookies and be with us and support us.

Everyone, it makes me happy to see you all here. Please start writing this in your hearts. The question we should ask today is not "*Lamah*," "Why did this happen," but rather, "*Le'mah?*" "For what? What are we meant to *do*?"

Please don't let them die for nothing, please don't just go back to your daily lives after the *shiva* (seven-day mourning period) is over. Take Rina and Maia as your inspiration to be better, otherwise their death was worth nothing. Don't let that happen.

There was so much light in Rina and Maia. If everyone here will remember Maia and Rina, and take some of their light and put it into practice, we'll bring the final redemption soon…

We need to believe and pray for miracles and break down the gates of heaven until the Temple is rebuilt and the dead return to life so I can see you again.

Thank you God for leaving me with Daddy, Keren and my Yehuda baby.

Maia, watch over Rina for us, and Rina please watch over Maia.

Lucy Dee's 7 F's

Lucy Dee often spoke of the "7 F's," the seven questions she would ask herself every day, and which she would regularly discuss with her family and friends.

FRIENDS — How am I treating my friends? How are my friendships going? Which relationships need work?

FAMILY — How am I treating my family? Who should I spend more time with? Who needs my attention and extra focus right now?

FITNESS — Am I up and about? Running? Exercising? Am I taking care of myself physically?

FAITH — How is my religious and spiritual growth? How is my relationship with God? Which areas can be strengthened?

FUNCTION — How am I fulfilling my calling in life? What needs to be done that only I can do? Am I living up to my potential?

FINANCES — Are we financially secure? Should we work less? Do my purchases reflect my values?

FLAME — What am I passionate about? What am I living for that feeds my soul? What is making me feel most alive?

Reflections from a Friend

Shira Marili-Mirvis

Rina Dee had a special necklace; on one side of the pendant it said "the world was made for me," and on the other side, "I am dust and ashes." The first time I noticed what it said on the pendant I thought to myself, "What 15-year-old girl wears such a necklace?" Immediately after that I thought, "What special parents buy their child such a necklace?"

Through my daughter Yuval, a childhood friend of Rina's, I had the privilege to meet Rina, as well as her mother Lucy and sister Maia, who were all murdered in the horrible terror attack in the Jordan Valley. They were a great light in the world. Memories of these special women keep circulating through my mind.

It's the afternoon. My daughter Yuval and her friends are in the kitchen, cooking. Rina is standing by the table chopping vegetables for a salad. She is telling us how messy her room has become because she broke down a wall. "What did you do?" I ask, not understanding. "I broke a wall," she says again, and laughs. "My room is next to my sister Tali's, and every time I wanted to speak to her I'd have to go around. So we broke down the wall. Now we share one big room together."

It is two days before Passover. We are knee-deep in bleach and cleaning, the house is more messy than organized. Yuval says, "Rina called, may I go up north?" After a chain of promises - she will update me at every stage, she will not hitchhike, she will only take buses, she will not go anywhere alone - Yuval quickly packs a bag and leaves to go hiking with three other friends. I hear about another girl who wanted to join but her mother was nervous. Rina sent her a message, trying to convince her to say yes: "it'll be amazing. In life, you have to trust God. And yourself. And hike around Israel. And camp out in incredible places because we're not going to get to do it after we get married. And you only live once."

During the long trek up north, after reaching the Golan heights, Rina noticed that the sun was about to set. She rushed to the driver and asked him to please stop the bus so that they could get a chance to pray the afternoon prayer. The girls got off the bus, prayed together and then took a selfie with the setting sun. "That's how it is with Rina," my daughter explained to me. Rina was careful to pray three times a day.

When Rina began her studies at the girls' high school in Kiryat Arba, she was surprised to find out that *Mincha* (afternoon prayer) was not part of the day's schedule. Each girl was welcome to pray in her free time but Rina refused to accept this. She spoke to the administrators until the school made a special slot in the schedule for *Mincha*.

An hour after they accompanied Rina to her final resting place, the girls got up from the circle they were sitting in at the funeral home. Without a word, without searching for a *minyan* (quorum of 10 men), they went outside in small groups, each found a corner, and prayed the afternoon prayer. We mothers stood there a distance away, keeping an eye on them, and said to ourselves: "This is the legacy that Rina has left them."

It's Friday, late morning. We are hiking on a trail not far from home. Yuval calls. I hear the sound of crying, a crying I have never heard before. "Mom, they killed my Rina." I tell Yuval that we don't know yet and don't have details yet, and that what we need now are prayers. I ask her to gather her friends and recite *Tehillim* (Psalms) together. Almost an hour later, I enter our living room. Rina's friends are crying and calling out to the heavens. They are reciting Psalms together: crying and also laughing.

We are saying Rina's chapters, they explain:

"Light is sown for the righteous, radiance for the upright."

"Sing to the Lord a new song, for He has worked wonders."

"A psalm of thanks. Raise a shout for the Lord, all the earth."

After one of the terror attacks two years ago, the girls took upon themselves to recite Psalms. They divided the chapters among themselves so that they each have set chapters to recite, and together they finish the entire book of Psalms whenever extra prayers are needed. Rina's chapters, which she recited over and over again, were Psalms 96 to 100; Psalms of thanks and praise to God.

They are laughing in between their tears. "Look at these chapters Rina has left us. She left us no choice but to say a psalm of thanks for the ascension of her soul."

From the moment the terrible news was heard in our town, a WhatsApp group was created for women, where each woman posts which chapters of Psalms she has said, and together they finish reciting the Book of Psalms over and over again. The numbers indicating how many times the book has been completed changes rapidly. At first the group was called "Psalms for the recovery of Leah bat Tzipporah (Lucy) and for the souls of Rina and Maia." After Lucy's death, the description was changed to "Psalms for the souls of Lucy, Rina and Maia." The speed with which the Book of Psalms was completed again and again did not change; hundreds of women from Efrat - friends of Lucy's, mothers of friends of the girls', women who never met the Dee family - continued to pour out their hearts and their tears in prayer through the Psalms.

For days after her death, we listened to messages that Rina had left us. In them we would hear her rolling laughter, her quick way of speaking, her common sense and her love for planning in advance. We were reminded of the personal responsibility she would shoulder, the initiative she would take and the hiking and volunteering she would participate in whenever she could, sometimes even when she wasn't supposed to.

Despite taking the highest levels of math, English and physics, Rina still found time for extracurricular activities. She volunteered for *Hashomer Hachadash* (an organization to help safeguard the land of Israel and help Israeli farmers) and helped establish an additional Ezra youth group in a new neighborhood in Efrat. She recruited girls to join the youth group and planned activities. Together with Adi, a fellow counselor, they quickly doubled the number of girls who joined the group. The girls were drawn to Rina's captivating laughter, the personal attention she would give them and the depth of her messages, while always wearing big glasses and an even bigger smile.

A month before her death, Rina contacted a counselor she had had in the past and asked if they could meet. When they sat together one morning, Rina told her: I feel like I'm not living enough, like I could do more. The counselor laughed. In addition to everything you're already doing? Ezra, school, volunteering? But she understood that Rina was serious.

Lucy was a brilliant woman with a fabulous sense of humor through which she managed to make us, the other parents, loosen up regarding our teenage daughters. She was a diligent and thorough woman. She was always ready to go out for a walk with friends, and she encouraged the girls to go out hiking and sleep outdoors in sleeping bags. In her special, gentle and honest way, thanks to very clear and deeply embedded values, everything was simple.

Lucy modeled a love for God and prayer, praying on time and setting aside time to study the Bible. It was Lucy who organized Torah classes for women on *Shabbat*.

Lucy loved singing *Shabbat* songs and managed to get her family to sing with her. The Dee women prayed *Kabbalat Shabbat* (the prayer to welcome the Sabbath) together at home, and then went as a group to the synagogue. The Dee women sang together during the meals. The Dee women became a tight knit group, thanks to Lucy.

After Maia and Rina's funeral, my sister told me that she had listened incredulously to the eulogies of the siblings and the father, Leo. She was deeply moved by their nobility, and their ability to say goodbye in the deepest, most personal way, while still meaningfully relating to the national level of the tragedy. I told my sister that I wasn't surprised; as someone who's had the privilege of knowing Lucy, I recognized the intertwining of a sense of humor and depth, standing firm on values and differentiating between what matters and what doesn't.

In my last back-and-forth with Lucy on WhatsApp, she thanked me for hosting the girls. I wrote back that they are simply incredible. In recent days I've heard many people ask: How do you raise children like these? The answer is simple: When that is the kind of person you are, the children observe and internalize your qualities and values.

On the *Shabbat* after the horrendous attack, dozens of teenagers crowded into our home. We ate together, spoke, cried and, most of all, we sang. We sang *Shabbat* songs that morphed into quiet, soulful songs. *When* Shabbat ended, my husband, Shlomo, told them that despite everything that has been happening in the country recently, he now feels calm. He sees that we have an amazing young generation. Our youth are deep, sensitive and caring. They pray from the depths of their souls and are lovingly connected to the people and the land of Israel. "With you," he said, "there is hope." The Jewish people live. *Am Yisrael Chai!*

Shira Marili-Mirvis is the rabbanit of the "Shirat HaTamar" congregation in Efrat. This article was translated from Hebrew.

Memories of Lucy Dee z"l

Caroline Peyser Bollag

As *Yom Haatzmaut* (Israel's Independence Day) approaches, my mind travels back exactly one year, to when we hosted the Dee family on *Yom Haatzmaut* at our home and the great time we had together. Over the past few weeks, we have heard so many wonderful things about Lucy, Maia and Rena, a"h (peace be upon them), and learned about their many outstanding and unique qualities. There is so much to admire about them and to apply to our lives.

Over the past few years we enjoyed so many fun and adventurous family get-togethers with the Dees, often together with a third family, the Junis family. These included multiple years of *Purim Seudah* (the festive meal eaten on the holiday of Purim), team-building games (ODT) over Hanukkah, paintballing during *Chol Ha-moed Sukkot* (Feast of Tabernacles), a group Bibliodrama workshop, *Yom Ha-atzmaut* (Independence Day) barbecues, dinner in the *Sukkah* (hut used on the Feast of Tabernacles), and shared *Shabbat* meals.

My three children are the same ages as the three oldest Dees, and that made for a natural connection. My oldest daughter Eden was friends with Maia during high school, and my youngest daughter Tova has been friends with Tali since elementary school. My son would hang out with Yehuda Dee during these family get-togethers, as they were the odd-men out in a group that consisted of 11 kids, 9 of whom were girls. As the only two boys among the three families, they found things to talk about despite their age difference.

Lucy was always up for a good time and interested in making holiday celebrations fun for her family. She loved connecting with people and joining together to celebrate. She would often reach out and ask: "Hey, what are you guys doing for holiday x?" A Whatsapp group would follow between our three families, to plan and figure out who was bringing what and who was making which game.

I remember *Purim* of last year, when our three families came together for the festive meal. Lucy brought her trademark pigs in blankets - both the vegetarian version for her two vegetarian kids as well as one of mine, and a meat version. She made sure to always have gluten free, vegetarian and carnivore options at every meal to accommodate the various preferences of her family.

We all love games, so no get together was complete without a few. That year Leo had made some kind of a Bible trivia game related to *Purim*, some of it a bit esoteric, which he was happy to explain to the group when almost nobody could solve the whole thing.

Since all of our children were teenagers, we also played a role-reversal game in which we presented typical parent-teen conflicts. The parents acted out how their own kids would act, and the kids got a chance to imitate how their parents would react to a given scenario. It was hilarious and enlightening.

When a meal was hosted at the Dees, they would inevitably invite some people who were new to Efrat or who might not have had another place to celebrate the holiday. They were always on the lookout for who might need an invitation and a place to feel included. Their attitude was: the more the merrier. If we had extra company with us, Lucy would tell me to bring them along. And whatever the holiday, Lucy came prepared - a relevant Torah / historical Kahoot game, relay races, or a virtual "escape room."

When we were together with the Dees, the table was bursting with conversation. The kids got along famously and my husband and I would chat with Lucy and Leo. Leo would always share a Torah thought or his unique perspective on current events, armed with lots of facts and statistics, and Lucy and I would catch up on what was going on in our lives.

Over the past year, Lucy and I walked together one morning a week, whenever we were both free and the weather cooperated. Lucy loved to exercise, and to do it while catching up with a friend was even better. We'd often talk about raising teenagers and the different challenges that arise. Lucy would love to hear or share a Torah thought and then think together about how she could turn it into a conversation starter to engage her kids at the Shabbat table.

She put a lot of thought into her parenting and into providing her children with enriching and meaningful experiences. The week before Passover, I reached out to the Dees to get their question sheets that they had everyone fill out in preparation for a thought-provoking, relevant, and meaningful *Seder* (the special meal on the first night of Passover). I was looking for ways to get our kids and guests more involved and I knew the Dees would have some great and creative ideas.

The last contact I had with Lucy was a Happy Passover GIF that she sent before the holiday. Lucy loved to send GIFs to her friends.

About a month before Passover we went to the Dees for lunch on *Shabbat.* My daughter Eden didn't come because she woke up feeling sick. Maia was disappointed, but Lucy cheerfully said, "So you'll see each other next time."

We could not have imagined then that there would not be a next time.

Through the loss of Lucy, Maia and Rina, I realize more acutely how each and every person is an entire world, and how much there is to treasure, admire and appreciate in the friends we take for granted and assume will always be there. While we hope to continue the traditions of shared family get togethers going forward, there will always be a gaping and painful hole left by their absence.

May their memories be a blessing.

Maia Stuck with Her Friends, Her Goals, Her Ways and Her Word

Atara Shmell

In the Book of Ruth, Naomi repeatedly tells her daughters in law, Ruth and Orpah, that they should not continue with her on her path back to Bethlehem. "Go back, my daughters," she says three times. Orpa evaluates the situation and realizes that if she goes with Naomi she will be a poor foreigner in a foreign land, and understandably turns back. But Ruth? She doesn't care that Naomi doesn't think she should join; she doesn't care that Naomi has nothing to give her. Ruth decides to stick with Naomi through thick and thin and is not willing to leave her: "Ruth clung to her."

The Hebrew root ד.ב.ק. means to stick together, to not leave, to not let go, and to keep holding on tight. This root appears in the Book of Ruth four times, relatively often. This root, more than any other, reminds me of Maia. To me it represents her personality.

Maia stuck to her friends. After a long period during 11th grade in which our friendship lapsed, Maia caught me alone one time and sadly asked me: "What's with our friendship? Are you interested in it at all?" I mumbled a response, not quite knowing what to say. But then I caught myself and apologized, because I realized I never really wanted to lose one of my best friends. I tried to explain my feelings and what had been going on. Maia, as a good, smart friend, let go of the past and forgave me. She then told me in no uncertain terms that in order to maintain and strengthen our relationship we need to work on it. We need to meet more often and not only wait for chance encounters. We need to plan and do different things together. Maia didn't drop our relationship even though I was ready to give up so quickly, and I thank her for that. From then on, our friendship flourished. She stuck to her friends.

Maia stuck to her goals. When Maia decided to do something - she did it! When she first made *Aliyah* (moved to Israel), Maia didn't give up until she fully became part of our class. She chose to acclimate culturally and tried to become friends with everyone. She even got a great grade on her Hebrew matriculation examination! She became Israeli in the best way - with British touches. Maia didn't rest. She chose her targets and went after them: she tried to be the best counselor in our youth group, worked long hours to decorate our *snif* (youth group clubhouse), studied hard to get the highest math grade she could, and argued with teachers for every point on tests. Maia pushed herself, and stuck to her goals.

Maia stuck to her ways. Recently, Maia kept telling me how I was a bad influence. While I served only one year of national service, she planned on doing two! She was trying to convince her parents and get them to agree, and I was proving to be a bad example (although I know they really supported her decision and were so proud of her). On trips up north with friends in the summer, when there are plenty of teenagers all trying to get on public transportation, Maia would politely push to get on buses, knowing exactly where to stand to make sure she got on the bus. She would pleasantly push to get through long lines at movie theaters, and to make sure that she, together with her friends, got in. She stuck to her ways.

Maia stuck to her word. She said what she meant and she meant what she said. Maia told the truth even though sometimes it wasn't so pretty. As a friend, it was an interesting experience. On the one hand, I could trust her word implicitly. On the other hand, she had no problem telling it as it is, straight to your face. When I think about Maia now, that's what I loved about her. She didn't run away or hide behind niceties, she said it like it was and she stuck to her word.

When Maia was taken from us on Passover we had just stopped asking for the winter's rain in our prayers, replacing the request with a statement that we now count on God's sustenance through the summer's dew. Maia's father explained that Maia's name meant the "water of God." God provides for us in different ways; sometimes with strong thunderous rains, and at times only with a light layer of dew. Even though Maia is no longer with us, I know that her presence and impact will continue to nourish and sustain us in different ways.

I hope I retain those lessons gleaned from Maia's special traits. I hope all of us, her friends, can continue to stick together and spread her light in this world.

Incongruities: The Roots of the Messiah

Atara Eis

As I grieve the unfathomable and brutal murder of my friend Lucy and her daughters at the hands of evil terrorists, I find myself flashing back and trying to remember every detail of my last conversation with her. It took place a week before the murders, as we celebrated the coming of age of our friend's daughter at her Bat Mitzvah party. We caught up after a few years of less consistent connection, spurred by the confluence of pandemic disruption and the birth of my sixth child. In our last conversation on this earth, I told Lucy that I was ready to return to the weekly women's Torah class that she helped organize, and that she could start bugging me to attend again. And we talked about how quickly our children were growing up and how proud she was of each of her children. We took a photo, in which she is wearing that gorgeous dress that has now, sadly, become known to millions.

I mourn the invitations for connection that Lucy and Leo extended to us throughout the years, to join them for this or that event or just to get together. Our very last *Shabbat* meal with friends before the first Covid lockdown was with the Dees.

I'm trying to be gentle with myself as I grieve their murder. It's ok that I'm overanalyzing every text message we ever sent. There will never be another text message, so I'm searching for inner meaning in the finite texts between us. It's understandable that I'm filled with regret for not answering enough of her invitations, for being too busy. There won't be another one. But she always understood! She told me she knew what the busy baby / little ones phase she had exited a few years before me was like. And so, her very last text to me, "enjoy family time," is seared in my heart. I'll do that for you, Lucy. I'll do my best.

I probably should stop searching for the omni significance of every text and email between Lucy and me, but Bible study is all about searching for omni significance in the infinite Biblical text, and so I'll seek solace in that. We live in Efrat, also known in the Bible as Bethlehem (literally, "House of Bread"), the location of the Ruth story. So gleaning the harvest story for hope and extra meaning during this time of grieving is only natural.

In the Ruth story, a wealthy family chooses to leave Bethlehem during a time of famine for Moab, a place known to be inhospitable and unkind. They return bereft of their men; one bitter mother-in-law with one foreign daughter-in-law, landless, destitute and poverty-stricken. It's the story of a plot gently hatched between Naomi and Ruth which, at first glance, should make us blush. For Naomi sends Ruth to beg for food in a field of male workers, and then to proposition its wealthy owner.

Rabbi Yaakov Medan points out the jarring contrast between the law in Leviticus forbidding sexual relations between a man and his sister-in-law, and that of a levirate marriage which requires precisely that which is generally forbidden, in the event that a man leaves behind no children. In the words of the tradition, these statements were said "in one utterance." They are complete opposites, but they intentionally coexist. This mechanism speaks to the deepest contradictions in life with which we must live. It creates this redemption story, which does no less than plant more seeds for the Davidic dynasty, as Boaz and Ruth's great grandson is King David himself. But the very acts that lead to field redemption and levirate marriage in order to redeem the soul of a childless man would be considered infidelity or prostitution in any other context. Everything is turned on its head! And yet, in this topsy-turvy context, the roots of the Messiah dig deeper.

Only hours before celebrating the miraculous splitting of the sea on the seventh day of Passover, we buried our friend Lucy. The night before the burial, after Lucy had succumbed to her wounds and her healthy organs were donated and used to save many other lives, our community gathered to grieve and strengthen each other through song and Torah lessons. I'm a perfectionist and rarely like to speak on the spot. It's something Lucy gently called me out on: "Nobody cares if your lecture is perfect or your attendance to other's lectures is perfect. Just get up and speak." So, I stood up and spoke.

I shared the verse in Exodus (13:17), which tells us that God didn't take the Children of Israel out of Egypt the easy way, using the shorter route. It would have been too easy to go back to servitude if the exit route got messy, as it undoubtedly would and did. Similarly, the Babylonian Talmud (*Eruvin* 53b) tells the story of a man who approaches a city and sees a child. "Which path do I take to the city?" he asks. The child responds: "There is a short path which is long, and a long path which is short." Take a look at a Family Circle cartoon where the mom calls the child home, and the child takes a nonsensical path home. Only a child can understand that sometimes, the longer path toward redemption is the shorter path. (Yes, children are usually impatient, but somehow, when they have to get from point A to point B, they are anything but efficient!).

We can't understand what happened to Lucy, Maia and Rina. All we see is injustice. We see people who are unable to discern basic right from wrong. We can't possibly see, from this human perspective, how anything here is good - and that's even with the unbelievable faith Rabbi Leo Dee has projected and shared with us. Nothing justifies cold blooded murder of purely innocent humans. But the long road is short.

The roots of Messiah are filled with incongruities, of which only God can make sense. Our job, meanwhile, as we await the redemption, is to act like Boaz, Naomi and Ruth, and like our modern-day Dee heroines. We must sow kindness wherever we go.

We NEED Lucy Back

Nechama Davis

Lucy and Leo's life was "thought through," in the sense that it is used in Ethics of the Fathers chapter one: "Be deliberate in your judgment." At every stage of their journey, they deliberated and considered, "What, as a Jew, should I be doing?"

It all began at a *Tikkun Leil Shavuot* (an all night Torah study program during the Feast of Weeks) which Lucy was running at Oxford during her studies there. And it ended so tragically when they were living in Efrat. Lucy's life was bookended by these two significant "chapters" so closely linked to the Book of Ruth.

There were many stations along the way: marriage, a year of traveling the world seeing suffering and happiness in off-the-beaten-track places, young married life in St John's Wood, London, *Aliyah* to Jerusalem and then Efrat, a return to London to lead and inspire synagogue communities and, in 2014, back to their beloved Efrat.

They both changed careers multiple times. Leo moved from Engineering to Venture Capital to Communal Rabbinics and then, inspired by Lucy's commitment as a school teacher, he threw himself into becoming a dedicated teacher.

Lucy loved being a rebbetzin (wife of a Rabbi). She was a real "natural," with her warm and bubbly personality and her passion to share the beauty of a Torah-led life. When they returned to Israel, she decided to train and become an English teacher. By all accounts, she became a truly outstanding teacher, dedicated to helping build the whole person and not just teaching the language. She became a much-loved and admired colleague and educator.

Lucy had another passion: to create opportunities for women in our neighborhood in Efrat to attend inspiring Torah classes, some given in Hebrew and some in English so that no one would be excluded, both on *Shabbat* and during the week. She charmed and convinced many busy educators to give classes or to host them in their homes. During the COVID pandemic, she was so keen to resume the classes once it was possible that she set up her own garden as an outdoor venue for these classes.

Though she was a new immigrant to Israel, Lucy made her way into the hearts and lives of the local Israeli women, not just the other Anglo immigrants. Anyone who got to know Lucy felt they had a warm and real connection with her. I was witness to this particular aspect of her life in the heartbroken cries of women during those intensely painful days between the attack and her passing. The cry that was repeated was "God, we NEED Lucy back!"

But Lucy's greatest career was motherhood. She loved her children fiercely, like a lioness. She wanted them to grow and blossom and flourish, and she would do anything to encourage them. She asked people to tell her their parenting secrets so she could grow as a mother and raise even more outstanding children. She wanted them to be givers, and she taught by example. She also prioritized family time, especially on *Shabbat* and vacations.

Lucy was an agent for change: she changed her own life in many different ways, and then she went on to inspire her husband and children, her wider family, the members of her synagogue communities, her school pupils and the women of Efrat. And now she has inspired the entire world. She was a woman of considerable talents, both intellectual and interpersonal. She used every single one of them for the good of others, and we are all the richer for having had her in our lives.

May her memory be a blessing.

Nechama Davis, former Rebbetzen of Chigwell and Hainault Synagogue, Essex, UK, now lives in Efrat.

Song of Songs and Ruth: Two Forms of Love

Dena Freundlich Rock

On Passover, we traditionally read the Song of Songs, and then seven weeks later, on Shavuot, we read the Book of Ruth. Interestingly, both books are love stories, but as my friend Rivka Kahan has pointed out, they portray radically different pictures of love. Song of Songs is rapturous, passionate, and full of yearning, a yearning that is never quite fulfilled. In contrast, Ruth is a story of loyalty and devotion, of love that is rooted and continues even after death. It is a love story that begins with three widows. Even after Ruth's husband dies, she remains loyal and committed to his mother, Naomi. Boaz too acts out of responsibility. The entire construct of *Yibum* (levirate marriage) is based on a commitment to giving a lost loved one continuity even after they are gone.

Both books are part of the Hebrew Bible; both depictions of love are essential parts of our tradition. We read Song of Songs on Passover when our relationship with God is new and budding. As He miraculously saves us with the Ten Plagues and the Splitting of the Sea, we are infatuated with this new Protector in our lives. But it is an unstable relationship, in which, like the "beloved friend" in Song of Songs, we complain and withdraw every time there is a bump in the road. We don't yet trust this new relationship.

On Shavuot, we read Ruth. Our relationship with God has matured and we are now ready for a relationship built on trust, commitment, and responsibility. Like Ruth, we accept the Torah, submissively and yet willingly, humbly and yet proudly, committing ourselves for life and beyond.

Lucy Dee was a remarkable woman who embodied the traits of both of these books. Like the "beloved friend" of Song of Songs, she was passionate and animated. Like Ruth, she was a woman of tenacity, commitment, and conviction.

The particular setting through which I was privileged to get to know Lucy was the women's *Shabbat* afternoon class in the Zayit neighborhood of Efrat. Lucy was one of the most consistent attendees, never wanting to miss an opportunity to learn. During the COVID era, the class, like much of life, had to go on hiatus. Lucy was one of the most passionate and determined to get the class restarted as soon as regulations would allow, and her large, shaded yard became the regular home for the class during those weeks.

Once the restrictions were lifted entirely, rather than just go back to regular pre-COVID routines as most people did, Lucy reached out to me and asked how she could help with organizing the class. And so she and I began a partnership; my role was to arrange weekly speakers and Lucy's was to find hostesses. Lucy was always an optimist, always upbeat, always with a positive attitude. She wasn't one to wait for others to take care of something; she would jump in and ask what she could do to help.

Quite fittingly, the class has been renamed *The Lucy Dee Women's Shiur*, and the Bible study each week is dedicated to her honor and merit. I cannot imagine a more fitting tribute to Lucy, who was passionate about learning and about bringing community together through Torah.

It is now our turn to take on the mantle of Ruth, and continue Lucy's legacy even after her tragic death through initiatives like the women's class, the Dee Ethics of our Fathers Project, Rabbi Leo's Daily Gratitude Project, and this memorial volume. May her memory be a blessing.

Rabbanit Dena Freundlich Rock teaches Talmud at Midreshet Lindenbaum, and teaches weekly courses in Jewish law at Midreshet Torah v'Avodah.

A Microcosm of the People of Israel

Gael Grunewald

In the personal story of one Jewish family, the Book of Ruth encompasses the exile-redemption story of an entire people: Leaving Israel, life in exile, and the return to the Land. At the root of the story lies the understanding that no matter where we are in the world, the Jewish people have a country to which they can always return. Throughout this story, we are also exposed to the values that have preserved the Jewish people for thousands of years; the values of a tight knit community life, acts of kindness, mutual responsibility and respect for the other.

The Dee family, who recently lost their mother, Lucy, and her two daughters, Rina and Maia, to terrorism, is also a microcosm of the Jewish people. The Dees lived in the Diaspora, made *Aliyah*, and worked in education and spreading Jewish ideals. And after making the ultimate self-sacrifice, Rabbi Dee and his children displayed the noble, indomitable spirit with which one Jewish family upholds eternal Zionist and Jewish values - no matter the price.

A golden thread of kindness, gentleness and compassion runs throughout the Book of Ruth. I hope and pray that this golden thread will continue to bond the destiny of the Dee family to the destiny of the entire Jewish people, in Israel and beyond.

Gael Grunewald is Deputy Chairperson of the World Zionist Organization and Director of its Education Department.

From Moab and the UK to the Hills of Bethlehem:

In Memory of Lucy Dee hy"d

Rabbanit Shani Taragin

Nearly a month has passed since that fateful Friday of Passover when Lucy was critically injured in a terror attack near the Hamra junction in the Jordan Valley on her way to Tiberias. Terrorists fired on the car she was driving and then shot over 20 bullets at close range, killing her daughters Maia and Rina, who were in the car with her. Lucy was evacuated by military helicopter to Hadassah Medical Center in Jerusalem. Unfortunately, despite the heroic efforts of the medical team, she succumbed to her wounds three days later and was laid to rest next to her daughters in Kfar Etzion, across the road from my home in Alon Shvut. Thousands attended her funeral, alternating between songs and sobs. The heart-wrenching eulogies of her husband, Rabbi Leo Dee, and her surviving children, Keren, Tali and Yehuda, will not soon be forgotten.

When tragedy strikes here in Israel, we feel the pain on a personal level; every Jew is a family member. But certain losses hit even closer to home. I had the merit to learn regularly with Lucy since she made *Aliyah* (moved to Israel) in 2014, through Torah courses offered by the Women's *Beit Midrash* (study hall) of Efrat and Gush Etzion. She assiduously took notes so as not to miss a single word, and after each class would wait to say "thank you" and explain how that class would change her perspective and actions going forward. Bumping into each other in the supermarket, we would continue our Torah discussions in the fruit and vegetable aisles. As *Yom Yerushalayim* (Jerusalem Day) approaches, I recall how she would sit with friends at the annual Women's *Beit Midrash* Torah class and breakfast with tears in her eyes, appreciative of the opportunity to learn and celebrate only a few miles from our cherished city.

As I think of Lucy and remember her together with her close friends and neighbors, I am struck by numerous remarkable parallels between Lucy and another mother from the hills of Bethlehem: Ruth. Both Ruth and Lucy left their homelands, their birthplace and their families to come to the fields of Judea. They were not raised as observant Jews, but both Ruth and Lucy pursued lives of Torah observance. At the *shiva* (seven days of mourning), the daughter of the Torah educator who taught Lucy many years ago spoke about Lucy's unusual curiosity and commitment at the young age of twelve!

Having studied Asian and Near-Eastern Studies at Oxford, Lucy lived in Japan for a year while keeping Shabbat and the Jewish dietary laws, and later traveled the world with her husband Leo. She served as *rebbetzin* (wife of the rabbi) of the communities of Hendon and Radlett, and like Ruth the Moabite, her priority was her family and their well-being, instilling in her children the values of *Torat chessed* (kindness). Like Ruth, Lucy taught through example and devotion. Rachel Wilk, a close friend of Lucy's, said that Leo and Lucy insisted their children not only adjust to Israel but also become contributors to Israeli society, in synagogue, school, and especially in their youth organizations. Lucy modeled this way of life by regularly attending synagogue with her four daughters and organizing community events and Torah classes.

Lucy organized the weekly *Shabbat* Torah class in the Zayit neighborhood of Efrat. Her long-time Torah class partner and next-door neighbor, Annie Pomerantz, reflected upon Lucy as "a phenomenal teacher, making it into a mission to teach English and invest in her students. She never spoke *lashon hara* (derogatory speech about others). If she didn't agree, she wouldn't argue but remain quiet."

Caroline Peyser-Bollag, a family friend, remarked, "Lucy was always interested in making holiday celebrations fun for her family. She loved connecting with people and joining together to celebrate. Lucy would love to hear or share a Torah thought and then think together about how she could turn it into a conversation starter to engage her kids at the *Shabbat* table. She put a lot of thought into her parenting and into providing her children with enriching and meaningful experiences." Valerie Pessin described her as an "extraordinary hands-on mother" who was, in Elana Abelow-Kronenberg's words, "idealistic, an incredible wife and an extraordinary friend."

Rena May-Juni shared how touched she was when Lucy proactively reached out and befriended her soon after her *Aliyah* (move to Israel). "Lucy craved deep friendships and worked tirelessly to maintain these friendships, despite our busy lives as mothers and professional women."

Ruth was willing to sacrifice her past to provide Naomi with a future. Not only did she enable Naomi to safely return to the Land, but she also provided her with a child through Boaz to perpetuate her family. Like Ruth, Lucy left her homeland and became a vibrant member of the Jewish people in the land of Israel, committed to her family and community in the same hills of Judea. Both had struggles yet remained focused on building, surviving and thriving with relentless dedication.

Ruth could not have known the impact her loyalty and kindness toward Naomi would have on future generations. The sages explain that the story of Ruth was canonized to teach us the rewards bestowed upon those who perform kindnesses (*Ruth Rabbah* 2:14). Ruth's sacrifices were rewarded with her progeny as she became the "mother of royalty." Like Ruth, Lucy could not have known the impact of her sacrifice, a sacrifice that has inspired our entire nation.

"What can I do to honor Lucy's memory?" asked Rena May-Juni. "Be proactive in nourishing friendships, cherish every moment with my children, be forgiving to myself and others, encourage creativity, commit to physical fitness, harness my power as a woman to do good in the world, embrace my flaws and love my spouse and children unconditionally."

Ruth did not live to see her great-grandson rise to royalty and begin our people's messianic line. Yet after three millenia, we continue to learn from her and remember her as one of Israel's greatest women of valor. United as one family and one nation, we hope and pray that we will learn from Lucy's remarkable legacy. May we soon see the rewards of her sacrifice.

Why World Media Should Accept Leo Dee's Dare

Gil Hoffman

In the 11th century before the common era, a Moabite princess needed to make a decision. She could remain in her Moabite palace and live an easy life of prosperity. Or she could join the mother of her deceased husband as she traveled back to her homeland, the Land of Israel, and live in poverty. Ruth's decision to join her mother-in-law and glean leftover wheat in the fields in order to survive is even harder to understand in current society, in which money is often prioritized over all other values.

Thirty-one centuries later, many people still make that courageous and counterintuitive choice to sacrifice themselves financially to live in Israel. The family of Leo and Lucy Dee is a modern day example of an immigrant family who left behind relative prosperity to live meaningful lives in the Judean hills. Leo gave up prosperous work in the financial sector in London to live in Efrat, adjacent to the fields of Bethlehem where Ruth had gleaned.

In one of the unsung miracles of the Book of Ruth, her *Aliyah* to Israel got good press. When Ruth asked the local leader Boaz why he was treating her well, he answered: "I have been told of all that you did for your mother-in-law after the death of your husband, how you left your father and mother and the land of your birth and came to a people you had not known before."

To emphasize how miraculous it was that Boaz heard positive news about Ruth, the scripture uses a rare doubling of words, *hugayd hugad* ("It was surely told"), to describe what he heard about Ruth through the grapevine. The Dee family was unfortunately not as lucky with how their *Aliyah* was portrayed.

Not only did Leo Dee have to deal with the excruciating news of the murder of his wife Lucy and their children Maia and Rina in the Jordan Valley, he also had to handle how it was portrayed by the media in his native England. Media outlets around the world appeared to justify the murders by noting where the Dee family lived and died.

The media watchdog I head, HonestReporting, called out The Guardian for passively saying the victims had been "killed" as opposed to "murdered," and for stating the location of the deaths in order to justify them rather than pointing out that the perpetrator was a terrorist. An Associated Press headline did not identify the victims or the murderer: "Two killed in West Bank after Israel strikes Lebanon, Gaza."

Al-Jazeera took victim-blaming to a new level with its headline, "Two Israeli settlers killed in occupied West Bank shooting." The subheadline stated that "a deadly gun attack was carried out on a vehicle near the illegal Hamra settlement," dehumanizing the teenagers by implying the terrorist's goal was to harm the car. As HonestReporting repeatedly reminds our readers, by making excuses for why Jews are being murdered, the international media is complicit in the violence and fuels further unrest.

The one positive that has come out of the brutal murders of a mother and her two daughters is that the world has been introduced to Leo Dee, a brilliant orator, inspiring rabbi, loving husband and proud father. Realizing that he had been thrust into the spotlight against his will, Rabbi Dee decided to use his pulpit to spread goodness and to challenge the international media to cover Israel fairly. He called a press conference attended by the Reuters wire service before his wife was buried, and he interviewed with nine media outlets while sitting *shiva* (seven-day mourning period).

Rabbi Dee's message to humanity was: "never accept terror as legitimate, never blame the murder on the victims, and there is no such thing as moral equivalence between terrorist and victim. The terrorist is always bad." Dee dared the foreign press to stop criticizing Israel for existing. "Isn't that how the world media treats Israel?" he asked. "We build, they murder us, they destroy. [They say] it's your fault, since you built it in the first place."

Rabbi Dee's request to post Israeli flags on social media was readily accepted by Jews around the world. His more important call to cover Israel fairly met with less success. "World media: show me your true colors," he implored. "Do you really believe in moral equivalence? Will you continue to support evil by giving it a voice? Am I and my family really a threat to world peace? We who teach kindness and love? We who value life over anything else? Is this anonymous killer really justified? Is he progressing moral values and a future for himself? Come on! Wake up! Listen to your souls. Do you really believe it? Or does it just sell advertising space for material goods none of us really need?"

Dee's dare should become the baseline for media reporting about Israel from now on. Journalists from media outlets across the globe need to ask themselves before they file their reports whether they crossed that line. Unfortunately, CNN crossed that line by shamefully equating the deaths of Lucy, Maia and Rina with those of Palestinians.

Like the Dees, I came to live in the Jewish state hoping for a better fate for my family. Just like it was difficult for Ruth, it has not always been easy for us. I hope the international media will prevent the next tragedy by heeding the lesson of Leo Dee and reporting more responsibly.

Gil Hoffman is the executive director and executive editor of the pro-Israel watchdog HonestReporting, which monitors coverage of Israel in the international mainstream and social media.

Davidian Politics vs Machiavellian Politics

Rabbi Doron Perez

This essay is dedicated in loving memory of Lucy, Maia and Rina Dee, who were murdered in cold blood by Arab terrorists on the festival of Passover. May their beloved memory be for a blessing .

The Book of Ruth, traditionally read on the holiday of Shavuot, concludes with the birth of King David (Ruth 4:22). Our Sages maintain that David was born and also died on this festival. It is only appropriate to trace the lineage of Israel's greatest king, the great grandson of Ruth and Boaz, on this holy day.

Treatment of Political Enemies

The hallmark of David's legacy lies in his remarkable attitude to his political enemies. His forgiveness, forbearance and toleration of those who not only vehemently opposed him but went out of their way to harm him was extraordinarily unusual. Somehow, he possessed the strength, fortitude and humility to not only forgive them but to work to unify with them and the many tribes of Israel they represented. David chose national unity over tribal triumphalism and internal cohesion over partisan politics.

At the heart of David's greatness lay a deep and coherent ideology for how a leader should treat his political enemies, i.e., those who are part of the same nation but are one's ideological opponents. To best understand "Davidian" politics, it must be contrasted with the more commonplace type of Machiavellian politics which couldn't be more different, an approach that dominates much of the political arena in our time.

The Hallmark of Machiavellian politics lies in the vengeful and destructive way in which one treats one's political enemies. This mode of behavior has a cogent philosophical basis. It is rooted in an uncouth, un-Jewish mode of political interaction, in which lying and deception are virtues, undermining political opponents is desirable and political ends always trump moral means.

Machiavellian Politics

A 16th century statesman and diplomat, Machiavelli served his native Florence for 14 years. Forced into retirement when the Medici family seized power, he wrote works of history and drama, but his lasting notoriety is due to his most famous work, *The Prince*.

In this watershed work, which ultimately established him as the "father of political science," Machiavelli drew upon his personal experiences and political studies to argue that politics has always been conducted with deception, treachery, and criminality. Machiavelli maintained that successful politicians should not abide by normal standards of morality and ethics. For successful politicians, the desired end always justifies the means, no matter how brutal or unethical. Rulers who hope to maintain their hold on power must know no moral limits. They must lie and deceive as needed, and should torment, torture and murder political enemies with impunity if they wish to secure and sustain their leadership. Most famously, he notes that for a ruler, "it is much safer to be feared than loved."

In the decades after it was published, *The Prince* gained a fiendish reputation. By the end of the century, Shakespeare was using the term "Machiavel" to denote amoral opportunists, leading directly to our popular use of "Machiavellian" as a synonym for scheming villainy. Throughout the book, Machiavelli appears entirely unconcerned with morality, except insofar as it is helpful or harmful to maintaining power.

Davidian Politics

Diametrically opposed to Machiavellian politics is the political leadership of King David – what we have called "Davidian politics." During David's 40-year rule, he modeled a form of leadership so transformative that he has become known to posterity as *David HaMelech*, King David, "the" king par excellence. So extraordinary was his leadership that the longed-for, future leader of Israel, the Messiah himself, must be a direct descendant of David.

David's respect for his political adversaries was remarkable, and could not be more different from Machiavelli's ideal prince. While David was a warrior who fiercely fought the enemies of Israel, he was extraordinarily forgiving and consistently tolerant towards his political adversaries, a compassionate attitude his own senior military brass and tribal leadership struggled to understand.

On several occasions, King Saul attempted to kill his loyal servant David, yet David twice refrained from harming him, even though his own life was in danger and he had every right to kill King Saul in self-defense. David also showed remarkable forbearance and forgiveness to Abner ben Ner and Amasa ben Yeter, chiefs of staff of the armies that fought against David on behalf of Saul's kingdom and Absalom's rebel forces respectively. When Yoab surreptitiously murdered these men, David rebuked Yoab for his actions and publicly mourned them. When the Amalakite youth and brothers Ba'ana and Reichav joyously informed David that they had killed his political enemies – King Saul and Ish-boshet – David had them killed for daring to harm an elected king of Israel.

The National Unifier

What drove King David to show such unusual mercy to his political adversaries?

David understood that the main role of the king of Israel is to unite the people. David knew that killing Saul or taking vengeance against political enemies could lead to an irrevocable split amongst the already divided tribes of Israel. He desperately sought to overcome painful internal divisions between his tribe of Judah and the other tribes of Israel who appointed Saul and Ish-boshet as their kings. His lifelong goal was to heal the fractures of national society and forge a unified people.

The Book of Samuel, which in many ways is the book of David, stands out as the blueprint for Jewish political leadership. It was David who bent over backwards to ignore prior insults, grievances and wars and to forgive others for the sake of unity, overcoming the tribalism that had plagued the people of Israel for generations. And so it was David who laid the foundations for the Temple in Jerusalem, where God's presence could only reside among a people united as one.

In both Israel and around the world, we are today in desperate need of the Davidian mode of Jewish leadership. May God grant us such leaders who will unite our people and rebuild the Temple, speedily in our days!

Rabbi Doron Perez is Chairman of the World Mizrachi Movement.

Discussion Questions

Shira Schechter, Content Editor of The Israel Bible

The Book of Ruth is a story of resilience, kindness, and redemption, all messages that we have heard from Rabbi Leo Dee since the tragic murder of his wife Lucy, and daughters, Maia and Rina. The Book of Ruth can help us think more about how to react in the aftermath of their devastating loss.

1   According to the Talmud (Bava Batra 91a), Elimelech was punished for abandoning the Land of Israel, and his children were punished for staying in Moab even after their father's death.

     The Dee family, on the other hand, moved to Israel from the UK. Since the deaths of Lucy, Maia and Rina, Rabbi Leo Dee has expressed that he has no regret about moving to Israel, despite the tragic deaths of his wife and two daughters, and has encouraged people around the world to show solidarity for Israel by posting pictures of Israeli flags on social media. He has also encouraged Jews worldwide, especially leaders of the Jewish community, to move to Israel.

What are some ways that you can show support for the State of Israel and those who are living in Israel? What can you do to encourage others to stand with Israel?

2   The Book of Ruth begins with the words: "And it was in the days when the judges judged" (Ruth 1:1). The period of the judges was characterized by a lack of leadership, as it says in the Book of Judges, "In those days there was no king in Israel; everyone did as he pleased" (Judges 21:25). The Book of Ruth ends with the birth of King David and the Jewish monarchy.

What can we learn about leadership from the Book of Ruth? How might the institution of monarchy be a solution, or a resolution, to some of the issues that arise in the Book of Ruth?

Lucy, Maia and Rina Dee were all leaders in their own ways. Lucy Dee trained to help new mothers and would visit and support them weekly in her hometown of Efrat. Maia was doing national service by volunteering in a high school, and Rina was a counselor in her local youth movement.

In what ways are you a leader? What can you get involved in, and what initiatives can you undertake, in order to make a positive impact on the world and on others?

3   Rabbi Zeira teaches that the Book of Ruth was written in order to teach the great reward for performing acts of loving-kindness.

How many examples of kindness can you find in the story of Ruth? Who performs each of these acts of kindness and who is on the receiving end of each one? What is the great reward that they receive for these acts of kindness?

It is said that doing kindness benefits not only the receiver but also the giver. How did everyone in the story benefit from kindness?

The Dees have always been known for the kindness and love that they show to others, and for their home which is always open to everyone. How can we honor the memory of Lucy, Maia, and Rina through acts of kindness? How can we ensure that their legacy of love and compassion lives on, even in the face of tragedy?

4   Naomi experiences the trauma of losing her entire immediate family and all of her wealth. Ruth becomes a foreigner in a foreign land who is shunned by most of her new neighbors. She is constantly called a Moabite, and the closest relative who is eligible to redeem her does not want to marry her lest he "ruin" his estate (Ruth 4:6).

How did loving-kindness help them each overcome their individual traumas? How can we use loving-kindness to help people that we know, like the Dee family, who are going through a difficult situation?

5   The Book of Ruth takes place during the time of the Judges, a period of instability and moral decay in Israel. The story highlights the struggles of ordinary people during this chaotic time, and how acts of kindness and faith can make a difference even in the darkest times. Lucy, Maia, and Rina were victims of a senseless act of violence that shattered their community and left many people feeling lost and vulnerable. The story of Ruth and Naomi can remind us that even in times of grief and uncertainty, there is hope for healing and renewal.

How can we use the story of Ruth to find comfort and healing after experiencing loss and trauma? What messages of hope and resilience can we take from the story, and how can we apply them to our own lives?

Family Dee Photos